MY BURDEN IS LIGHT

MY BURDEN IS LIGHT

SUFFERING AND CONSOLATION IN THE CHRISTIAN LIFE

SAINT JOHN OF AVILA

Compiled and Translated by
Brandon Otto

TAN Books
Gastonia, North Carolina

Translated by Brandon P. Otto

Cover design by Jordan Avery

Cover image: *Christ Embracing St. Bernard* by Francesc Ribalta. In the Public Domain via Wikimedia Commons.

ISBN: 978-1-5051-3343-1
Kindle ISBN: 978-1-5051-3497-1
ePUB ISBN: 978-1505-1-3496-4

Published in the United States by
TAN Books
PO Box 269
Gastonia, NC 28053
www.TANBooks.com

Printed in the United States of America

Contents

Introduction

Prayer is warfare to the last breath.
—Abba Agathon[1]

THE yoke of the Christian life is easy, for it is not borne alone: God Himself bears it with us and for us, so that He can carry us up the mountain of holiness like a little child, in St. Thérèse's image. Yet this yoke is Jesus's yoke, and so it must needs have splinters and thorns.

Despite God's aid, the Christian life is still always a struggle, always suffering. We, like Jesus, must deny ourselves, take up our cross, and follow Him.[2] It is a pilgrimage, and a pilgrimage, although joyful, is never easy. A pilgrim is a stranger in a strange land,[3] without a roof to call his own, for here he has no lasting city, but he looks for the one to come.[4] As he hikes the star-way to Heaven, he encounters battles, ambushes, and enemy warriors and tricksters, and he wages a war for his soul against them. Warfare is tiring work, and the pilgrim grows drowsy, so he needs the aid and example of fellows to keep him awake, to keep him on watch, to keep him vigilant. With their aid, he shall come to the Jerusalem on high, and even the suffering his pilgrimage gave him will be celebrated with joy, because of where it led him.

---

1 Agathon #9 in *The Sayings of the Desert Fathers: The Alphabetical Collection,* tr. Benedicta Ward (Kalamazoo, MI: Cistercian Publications, 1975), 22.

2 See Mt 16:24.

3 See Ex 2:22.

4 See Heb 13:14.

These are the things St. John of Ávila preaches to us in the sermons translated here: the Doctor of the Church becomes a Doctor of our souls, binding us up when robbers befall us on our pilgrimage. And this skill, of course, is not his own: he is merely an apprentice of the true Soul-Doctor, Christ.

Jesus, our Doctor, is also our Captain, our *avant-garde*, who went forth and suffered these things before us, for our example. St. John first tells us of this war against "the world, the flesh, and the devil," this war in which we labor as soldiers in the vineyard; then he tells us of our Captain, who bested the devil in the desert, yet, through His love for mankind, was bested by a woman's prayers. Next, he tells us of our Captain's processions, His sorrowful pilgrimage on earth, followed by the triumphal procession of His Eucharistic Body, when "the Unarmed makes war, / And the Slain hath the gain."[5] Finally, St. John shows us other veterans of this war, to inspire us: Mary, who conquered God in prayer even as a child; St. Francis of Assisi; and St. Catherine of Alexandria.

"Great is the struggle of prayer, when one strives to always keep his mind fixed on God with a stable intention, despite the enemies opposing him and snatching the sense of prayer away to [chase after] various things."[6] Great is this struggle, and great the sweat and blood we shed in it, yet "the clods of battlefields are red / with immortality."[7] The Christian's struggle in this life leads him along the bloody footsteps of Christ, which bring him to the eternal rest Christ won for us.

The Christian's life is "a fight to the death in everything and even in all trifles,"[8] and it is to this fight that St. John calls us here. But

---

5 Francis Thompson, "The Veteran of Heaven," in *Complete Poetical Works of Francis Thompson* (New York: Boni and Liveright, Inc., n.d. [1918]), 117.

6 Origen, *Commentary on the Epistle to the Romans* X.15 (PG 14:1277B).

7 Charles Dalmon, "Stanzas from 'Elegy for Edward Thomas,'" in *Poems of Our Time: 1900–1960,* ed. Richard Church, Mildred Bozman, Edith Sitwell (London: Dent, 1967), 108.

8 Elder Michael of Valaam, qtd. in Maria Stakhovich and Sergius Bolshakoff, *Interior Silence: Elder Michael: The Last Great Mystic of Valaam,* ed. Abbot

though we must put in our own struggles, like the martyrs—whom the Coptic Church calls "struggle-bearers"[9]—we are not alone and unaided. Our Captain has not gone on to His rest and abandoned us: He is still with us in the trenches of life. So, though "only for manly warfare are crowns given," our manly effort is only our little offering, for it is Christ who is the true warrior of light: "Arm yourself and wage war, and everything else will be given you by the Lord."[10]

St. John's sermons show us the example of our Captain and of His brave warriors, and they call us on to zeal and hope in the struggle of the Christian life. They call us to wake for war, a war we have already won, for Christ has won it for us.

Wake now, wake now!
War is kindled.
Now helm to head,
to hand the sword.
Wake now, warriors,
wielding glory![11]

Brandon P. Otto

Herman (Ouzinkie, AL: New Valaam Monastery, 1992), 108.

9 The Greek term is ἀθλοφόρος (*athlophoros*). The first half of the word can either mean "prize" (ἆθλον, *athlon*) or "struggle, contest" (ἆθλος, *athlos*). Most dictionaries follow the first option, making the full term mean "prize-bearer" or "prize-winner," while the Copts opt for the second option, yielding "struggle-bearer." See, for instance, the Coptic common hymns for male martyrs in *Service of the Deacons: Rites and Hymns of the Liturgies and Services of the Coptic Orthodox Church* ([Houston, TX]: Coptic Orthodox Diocese of the Southern United States, 2010), 222–226.

10 Elder Michael of Valaam, qtd. in *Interior Silence,* 122.

11 J.R.R. Tolkien, "The Lay of Gudrun" §99, in J.R.R. Tolkien, *The Legend of Sigurd & Gudrún,* ed. Christopher Tolkien (Boston, MA: Houghton Mifflin Harcourt, 2009), 286.

Translator's Note on the Text

THE source I have used for this text is the compilation of sermons found in the 1953 critical edition of St. John's works: *Obras Sermones del B. Mtro. Juan de Ávila : edición crítica,* Tomo II : *Sermones. Pláticas espirituales,* ed. Luis Sala Balust, Biblioteca de Autores Cristianos (Madrid : La Editorial Católica, S.A., 1953). Sala Balust gathered the sermons from various sources, sometimes previous publications, sometimes manuscripts, collecting eighty-two sermons in all, though St. John certainly wrote many more, now lost.[12]

For the sermons translated in this volume, Sermons 8, 9, 10, and 16 were first printed in Ricardo García-Villoslada, "Colleción de ermons inéditos del Beato Juan de Ávila," *Miscelánea Comillas* VII (1947), 76–92, 39–49, 64–75, and 285–291. Sermons 37 and 63 were originally labelled as "treatises" or "tractates" (*tratados*) when they were published in an early edition of St. John's works. Sermon 37 was the second in a series of twenty-seven "Treatises on the Most Holy Sacrament of the Eucharist," found in *Tercera parte de las obras del P. Mtro Juan de Ávila . . .*, ed. Juan Díaz (Madrid: P. Madrigal, 1596), I:45–94; Sermon 63 was the fourth in a series of eleven "treatises" on Mary and Joseph, found in the same

[12] During St. John's process of beatification in the 1700s, many volumes of his manuscripts were sent to the Vatican and then disappeared. A 1746 list of the writings in those manuscripts, prepared by the Sacred Congregation of Rites, is reprinted in *Obras completas del B. Mtro Juan de Ávila: edición crítica,* Tomo I: *Epistolario. Escritos menores,* ed. Luis Sala Balust (Madrid: La Editorial Católica, S.A., 1952), xxxiii–xxxv.

publication, II:269–294. Sermons 78 and 80 were newly edited by Sala Balust from manuscripts.

All sermon titles and sub-headings are provided by Sala Balust, not myself.[13]

Page numbers for the Spanish text of the sermons in Sala Balust's edition are as follows:

Sermon 8: 155–173
Sermon 9: 173–184
Sermon 10: 185–197
Sermon 16: 275–281
Sermon 37: 575–603
Sermon 63: 981–995
Sermon 78: 1210–1232
Sermon 80: 1243–1253

For Scriptural quotations, I have provided my own translations of whatever text St. John uses, be it the Vulgate, be it a Spanish translation or paraphrase. I have often consulted the Douay-Rheims for suggestions in translating texts from the Vulgate. For ease of reference, chapter-and-verse citations are based on the modern RSVCE rather than the Vulgate's or Douay-Rheims's numbering.

---

[13] The editor of the Spanish edition also italicized certain words and phrases throughout the text. This seems to have been done in instances where St. John was quoting directly from Scripture and when he wrote in Latin. The intentional italicization of words and phrases is retained in this translation.

Part 1

"Waging a War Which Regards Our Souls"

Sermon 8

Motives for Laboring in the Vineyard of the Lord

(Septuagesima Sunday, 1 Cor 9:24–27, 10:1–5; Mt 20:1–16)

"Voca operarios."
"Call the workers."[14]

Exordium: Laying Out the Parable

THE office of father of the household: he who has a house and estate and brings workers to labor *at it* has to—very much—pay the laborers the day's pay that he agreed to with them; he has to not defraud them in paying for their work. *He who spills the* blood of his neighbor *and he who does not pay the day's pay to him who has labored* in his estate sin equally, *they are brothers,*[15] the sacred Scripture makes them equal.[16] He who has an estate, in order to bring to it him who will take care of it and plow it, let him be ready to pay him his day's pay and labor. The burden of him who comes to labor is to faithfully do all that he can and to labor with diligence and care. The office of the wife, the office of the lady of the house, is to make very good stew to eat for those who come to labor

14 Mt 20:8.

15 This phrase is only found in the Vulgate's form of this verse, and only in certain manuscripts at that.

16 Sir 34:27 (DR).

on the estate of their husbands, so that, when they come tired, they might be refreshed and rest and laze about.

You see it, then, well laid out here. The lord of the vineyard is God; He is a very good, a marvelous employer.[17] *The seed of Jacob, no?*[18] *Did I speak in vain to the sons of Israel that they might serve Me?*[19] The interlinear gloss says: No, for He promises the kingdom of the heavens.[20] Complain about that employer over there. Does He pay you poorly for the labor you did for Him? The laborers are us. Such ones we are! May God make us better through His goodness and mercy. She who has to make stew is the Virgin, the bride of God. If we commend ourselves to her, doubtless she will hear us, for most great is the care she continually has for us. And thus the introit of the Mass says it: *They surrounded me*, etc.[21]

To call upon God is to distrust oneself and to trust in God, declaring one's tribulation. Call upon Him, for it will not be in vain, because He says in the temple[22] that He will hear you in the holy temple.[23] This temple is the Virgin, Our Lady; here He sat when He became man; here He dwells now by grace. Let us call upon Him in her, so that we might be good laborers, and that we might receive

---

17 More literally, "payer," or "one who pays."

18 *Numquid semini Jacob?*

19 Is 45:19.

20 *Non, quia promisit regnum caelorum. See Biblia sacra cum glossis interlineari et ordinaria, Nicolai Lyrani Postilla…* (Lyons, 1545), IV:79v.

21 *Circumdederunt me.* This sermon was given on Septuagesima Sunday, the third Sunday before Ash Wednesday and the beginning of the Pre-Lenten season. The introit of the Mass is based on Psalm 18:4–6: "Surrounded me the groans of death, the sorrows of hell surrounded me, and in my tribulation I called upon the Lord, and He heard my voice from His holy temple." See Gaspar Lefebvre, *The Saint Andrew Daily Missal With Vespers for Sundays and Feasts and Kyriale* (Great Falls, MT: St. Bonaventure Publications, 1999), 241, for the Latin I have translated here.

22 *In templo.*

23 Ps 18:6.

the denarius.[24] Let us beseech the sacred Virgin that she might gain us grace, and, so that she might so do this, let us say to her, with devotion, the Ave Maria.

The Epistle and the Gospels Invite Us to Labor

Call the workers . . . where aforementioned.[25] The words that, with the favor of the Holy Spirit, will give the foundation for our sermon, Jesus Christ said them in the Gospel which was chanted[26] in today's Mass. They say, in our tongue:[27] *Call the laborers and pay them the day's pay.*

It seems that the Gospel and the Epistle for today joined in harmony in order to tell us the one saying that we wouldn't want to hear. It seems they throw verjuice[28] in our eyes. The Gospel says that we have to labor in the vineyard; you already see what there is to do in it: it has to be pruned, broken open, dug, planted with vines, watered; there's much to do in it. The Epistle tells us another labor: that we have to fight and run. See by your limps how new you are! And not however you want, but better than others. *I run.*[29] Not this way, stopping and starting, here and there, but you have to run without ceasing. "Thus," he says, "do I fight and fence, thus do

---

24 A Roman silver coin. In the Gospels, it is used to represent a worker's daily wage.

25 *Voca operarios . . . ubi supra.* See Mt 20:8.

26 In the Tridentine Mass, the Epistle and Gospel were always chanted instead of simply read. The practice of chanting the Scripture readings continues today in the Eastern Rite Liturgies and occasionally at Masses, particularly large Masses at the Vatican.

27 Literally, "in a Romance language" (*en romance*), which typically means "in Spanish." A Romance language is one derived from Latin (the Roman tongue), such as Spanish, French, Italian, Romanian, etc. Recall that, in St. John's time, the Mass and its readings were recited entirely in Latin.

28 An acidic juice pressed from unripe grapes or other fruit; in St. John's time, it was often used in cooking in the same ways vinegar is used today.

29 *Ego curro.* 1 Cor 9:26.

I fight, *not as if punching the air.*"[30] The Gospel puts the sickle in our hands, and the billhook[31] and the hoe. The Epistle commands us to go forth to run, to fight, and to fence. The Gospel commands labor; we laze about. The Epistle [commands us] to fight; we want to be at peace. See how far it is from what He tells us to what we want, from what they command us to what we do!

Call the laborers, says the Lord; *to the laborers of the vineyard, give their day's pay.*[32] And he who has not labored? *None shall be crowned except he who has legitimately struggled.*[33] What remedy is there, so that we won't be so lazy? What remedy is there, so that we won't be as idle as we are and won't abhor labor as we abhor it? So the intent of our mother, the holy Church, is, this day, to invite us to labor and to advise us to not rest. Why such lazing about, brothers? Why such idleness?

The father of the household goes out. God is given many names: father of the household, lion, lamb, angel, heaven, water, fire, and many, innumerable other names. *Every name, both long and short*, said St. Bartholomew, according to what Dionysius recounts.[34] And He who has the vineyard, who has slaves, is called lamb, king, stone, fire, river. All that there is in creatures is affirmed of Him,

---

30 *Non quasi aerem verberans.* 1 Cor 9:26.

31 A curved blade on a small handle, used as a pruning tool.

32 Mt 20:8.

33 *Non coronabitur nisi qui legitime certaverit.* 2 Tm 2:5.

34 *Totum nomen, et longum et concisum.* This "Dionysius" is known by the lengthy name of "Psuedo-Dionysius the Areopagite." Modern scholars estimate the author is from the late fifth century or early sixth, though he claims to be Dionysius the Areopagite, one of Paul's converts (See Acts 17:34), and thus he claims to have known St. Bartholomew and to have been present at Mary's Assumption. His writings—both for their claim of antiquity and for their blending of Christianity and Neo-Platonism—were incredibly influential. Though he wrote a famous work entitled *On the Divine Names,* the quote here is actually derived from *The Mystical Theology* I.3: "Thus, then, the holy Bartholomew says that theology is much and least, and that the Gospel is wide and large, and, again, concise" (PG 3:1000B–C).

because in Him is the perfection of all of them, much more excellently than in themselves. On the one hand, the name of God Our Lord is *long*, and, on the other, *short*. There, they give Him the name of every servant, and, here, they find no name that fits Him. There, you give Him the being of all things, through the greater eminence that there is in Him; here, you deny it of Him: He is lamb, but not like that lamb; He is fire, but not like that fire. Then what [name] will you give Him, so that He might properly be the Lord, *He who is?* It cannot be said.[35] You see how short, you see how long and how wide, [God is].

In the Gospel, He is spoken of as the lord of the household. He comes at such an hour: "go out to my vineyard."[36] (Here he recounts the story of the Gospel until they came to paying the laborers.)[37] You see him, thus far, cautious in sending people out to labor in his vineyard; at night, you'll see him cautious in paying. (*He told the rest of the Gospel, how he made them all recline at table*,[38] and how he had them paid equally, and how those who had come first to the vineyard grumbled, and what the father of the household responded.)

In regards to this theme, I say: it is extreme goodness to draw good from evil; and, on the contrary, it is great evil to draw evil from good and goodness; the art and condition of the devil is to draw evil from good. God is, contrary to him, He who draws good from evil; His art and His property is to draw good from evil. *Is your eye vile because I am*

---

35 St. John is here using the arguments of "apophatic theology" or "negative theology," a specialty of Pseudo-Dionysius. Per apophatic theology, God is so great, so beyond our ken, that we come to know Him better by denying His relation to things we know than by making analogies and comparisons; as Dionysius himself puts it (*Mystical Theology* I.3), we can by "knowing nothing of Him, know Him beyond mind" (PG 3:1001A), Him Who is the "darkness beyond light" (*Mystical Theology* II.1, PG 3:1025A).

36 Mt 20:4.

37 This sermon was recorded by one of St. John's listeners, and here, as well as later in this paragraph, he simply summarized a few portions of the sermon.

38 *Dixit residuum evangelii, quomodo fecit omnes discumbere.*

good?[39] Your eye is evil, because I am good; in you is evilness, because I do good; to him I do mercy, and, to you, justice; *to no one do I do injury; I want to give him just the same as you. I will be equal with you, for I will give you a denarius; take it and go joyfully.*[40] What is it to you if I give as much to him who came at the end as to those who came in the morning? You are evil, for you are weighed down by the good I do, and I am good for doing it. Why can't I do good for whom I will?

So it shall be that the last shall be first and the first, last . . . many are called, and few chosen.[41] The Lord said this to him first, in order to let him understand that many who begin to serve God—because you do not take care—that many of these first ones are last: they will be thin and tepid and they will remain outside, and others, who began later, will go on ahead with the approval of devotion, although they came at the end.

"Lord,[42] since one works more than another, why do they give him an equal day's pay?" Those are the judgments of God. Those latecomers needed to labor with some quality with which the others did not labor; for approval in the service of God, knowledge in the School, does not come from a heap of years and works, but from living love, from that which is like mustard that burns, that has force and power within, in the fervor with which you act, in the intention with which you go aright, in the taste with which you appease Him. Thus He will recount how, by the grace of God, one who gives a

---

[39] *An oculus tuus nequam est quia ego bonus sum?* Mt 20:15.

[40] Mt 20:13–14.

[41] Mt 20:16, 22:14.

[42] St. John's sermons abound in these questions that he puts into the mouths of his listeners, or of a character he is discussing. The typical address these questions use is *Señor*. The word can mean "lord," both as in "the Lord" and as in "my lord"; it can also mean "Sir" or "Mister" (similar to the German *Herr*). It is not always clear whether St. John intends these questions to be directed towards him or towards Christ. For consistency, in these questions, I have always simply translated it "Lord," but one should keep in mind that it can mean either "Oh Lord" (addressed to Christ) or "my lord" (addressed to the preacher).

mite for God gives more than another who gives a great number of ducats;[43] a sigh that one gave in a corner [does more] than however many fasts and disciplines another does, day and night.[44]

It is a saying by Jesus Christ that Our Lord does not so much look on the gift as on the will and love with which it is given. Did He not say, when the old woman tossed a cornado[45] into the treasury, that *she had tossed in more than any of the rich*?[46] Our Lord looks more at the love with which you give, that difficulty you find in doing something and the labor you put into completing it and obeying Our Lord, that anxiety you have for fulfilling what He commands of you, that zeal for the honor of God that you desire to give Him—that is what God looks at, more than at another who, without love or liveliness, as if by custom, does it, without any further feeling, as if he were doing nothing; that one is not as acceptable to the Lord, nor does He pay him as much in abundance. The latecomers who came to labor had to repent, because they came late to the vineyard of the Lord, and they had to sorrow over how little they labored, and they had to labor with great anxiety and with a desire that the day would not end, in order to labor more, and [they had] to not look to what the Lord was to give them, but rather to preparing His estate and to contenting its Lord. And to these was given as much as to the others, and even, perhaps, more. The Lord says: *The last will be first and the first last, because many will be called and few chosen.*[47]

Many Are Called, Few Chosen

This is a difficult step. How is it to be understood? All those called today were called by the Church, and no one was cast out. How,

---

43 See Lk 21:1–4.

44 See Lk 18:9–14.

45 A small copper coin of St. John's time.

46 Lk 21:3.

47 *Erunt novissimi primi et primi novissimi.* Mt 20:16, 22:14.

then, does He say that *few* were chosen? All those who were called were chosen, and the called were many; later, the chosen were many. How, then, does He say, *Many are called and few chosen?* Those two words—*called* and *chosen*—must, necessarily, be mixed up.

The *called* are considered in the Scripture in two ways: *First*, those who are preached to, and whom God inspires so that they would amend themselves, and whom He invites so that they might come, and they neither come nor respond to the call of God. Thus, over there, on the borders, many were called and did not come; they are also called to whom God speaks, in their heart, about the evil life in which they walk and about what hinders them from the good, for their salvation, but they come to Him and know Him and remain here and ever dispose themselves so that God might help them and so that they might leave their evil life. There are *others* called, whom God inspires so that they would come at His call, and convert from their evil life, and walk on the way of God, and embrace, with love, that which fulfills them, and the Lord allows them to work and effect what befits their salvation.

God sends you a preacher who tells you what fulfills you, a good and holy proposition and a good thought; God has already done what is owed on His part.

"Father, what will I do, since I do not make use of this, since all that God has done for me has not caused any more cleanness in me than if He had not done it?" With this, God has already worked His justice, and when He comes to judgment with you, you will not blame Him for not having done His duty and all that was necessary to save you, if your evilness had not hindered it. There, He will ask you how you acted in regard to what was in your hand, how you made use of what you could do, and how you responded to Him, and if He finds some fault in you, He will severely punish you.

"Lord, if You do not give me another grace, it will be justice to condemn me; let Your Majesty grant me favors[48] in advance; in what has, unto now, done me wrong, I find myself wronged."

---

[48] The word *merced* typically means "mercy," though it can, confusingly, also refer to a royal grant, a gratuitous benefit, and even a rental payment. The

By your evilness, what God has done unto now becomes justice and condemnation and burden and obligation for you. Step forward and ask God that He be more lavish with you in favors and mercies. Say to Him: "Lord, do more for me, give me more, multiply Your mercy towards me. How? May You, Lord, open this heart and give me, Lord, the strength to want to do what You command of me and say that I must do; may You make me want what You want, and may I, although it be difficult, do what You want me to do. Give me, Lord, that second grace, which not only invites, but gives me to understand, gives me to eat, and makes me eat." That is what you have to desire, ask, and plead for, groaning and crying and laboring, although it cost you your life.

"Since it has to do with my will, how do you say that God will do it?"

That is God's wisdom and the love He has. He knows how to surround this in such a way that you will want it, because He acts so that you might want it and want it freely; this is called a call with effect, with execution, with building off of that *call* with which God calls you in the first calling. This is what Saint Paul signifies when he says: *Paul, called an apostle.*[49] Why do you say *called an apostle*? Because God inspired you so that you might exercise the office of the apostolate? This is not merely calling "come here," but saying and doing. *Called a saint*[50] is the same thing; *already made saints*, sanctified and justified and workers of goodness. More clearly: He called the wheat, the stars, the sun, *as is found in the first chapter of Genesis.*[51] And Saint Paul says that He calls that which is not as if it were, because He gives it being in His calling it; in God, to say is to do; God calls "just" those whom He makes justified and "holy" those whom He sanctifies and purifies.

Latin cognate—*mercedem*—is used to mean "wage" in Matthew 20:8. To keep the terms distinct, I am here translating *merced* as "favor" and *misericordia* as "mercy;" St. John likes to pair them, as in the next paragraph.

49 *Paulus vocatus apostolus.* Rom 1:1.

50 *Vocatus sanctus.*

51 *Ut invenitur Genesis primo.*

But there is a man who spent so much time flaying faces, hardened and forgotten. God says: "Here I want to do mercies for the exaltation of My Name and for My honor and so that My marvels be known, because [I will do them] to this man without owing it to Him, before He has made Me enraged, irate, and moved to do justice to him;" for God seeks the most wounded, the most sickened.

"Why, Lord, to this man more than to another? Look, Lord, at how exhausted he is from doing You affronts and injuries. Why this man?"

So that they may know that God is the Lord of what He has, and that they may know that what He gives is grace, and that the favor and mercy are what He wants to do, and what He gives and what He pays and all that He does for men is not a debt or a day's pay, and that He gives it to whom He holds as good, and, from whom He wills, He takes it away. That calling is a choosing as privilege, as by absolute power, in order to convert a dogged and hardened heart. He is lavish and very abundant in mercy and favors. This is the choosing that the Gospel speaks of. And so that we aren't careless about ourselves, and so we don't say to ourselves, "If we don't work at this hour of the morning, it'll be done at noon; if not, in the afternoon, and, if not then, then when the sun is setting"—this is not a good story; don't console yourselves with this—God says, "*Of them, few are chosen*; the called are many, but, from those, these ones are chosen." This manner of choosing is not done with everyone; there are few chosen in this manner. There are many who go along this way when God favors them, just as, by the second call of which we have spoken, many are those who are thus saved; but few are those to whom, by other particular privileges—they being of poor lineage, some being sinners—He gives better goods, does them mercies and greater favors; but *they are few*,[52] outside of the common way—we might say, "supernaturally." This happens very few times, this happens with very few, those thus called are very rare.

---

52 *Sunt pauci.*

So that you are not dismayed, brother, if you have badly wasted your life, ask God for mercy, and labor with diligence and with fervent desire and love; that little bit of time that remains for you, spend it in laboring towards God's coming to you, and in working in His Church, in your neighbors, in amending yourself, so that God will do you favors by choosing you among those few. You do not have to be so careless that you wait until the end, nor so dismayed that you never labor.

First Motive: We Will Avoid the Biting of the Conscience

Let's return to the theme. What will we do in order to not be careless, so lazy, so that this lazing about, this strolling through streets and sitting in chairs and being like slouchers, won't feel too good to us, being always idle, with no memory of labors, nor of discontent, nor of displeasure? What detours God takes to make us laborers, to entice us and draw us to the field to do something, to focus on some task! How many things stop us from laboring! What obstacles, what setbacks, what bitterness fall upon us in labor so that, in tasting it, we feel bad, and we throw it away! I said: Why don't you labor? "Because it is a pain and a labor to labor." And if you don't labor, will you be without pain and labor? Do you think that you'll laze about and that you'll rest? You've thus been called to the vineyard of the Lord, and are your hands folded? The vineyard is you yourselves, your soul, for God wants you to labor in it and to work it: *The vineyard of the Lord of Hosts is the house of Israel, and the man of Judah, its delightful seed.*[53] *The vineyard was peaceful.*[54] *In the Song of Songs, it is shown how every man is the vineyard of the Lord.*[55]

---

53 *Vinea Domini exercituum domus Israel est; et vir Iuda germen eius delectabile.* Is 5:7.

54 *Vinea fuit pacific.* Sg 8:11.

55 *In Cantica Canticorum probant quando quisque homo sit vinea Domini.*

What are you trying to say *when you say*: *My beloved, let us go to the field*?[56] Saint John said to Saint Paul: "Let us go out from among the Hebrews—since we make so little fruit—unto the Gentiles." Let us go out from ourselves, and let us go to the field of our vineyard, which is the Church, for everyone in this Church is her member, and she the body; because of that, they call you a part of the vineyard and the vineyard [as a whole]. You are the vineyard; come to labor in it; come to yourself if you want to know yourself. What are you trying to say? Come to your soul and do in it what is wont to be done in a vineyard, what a diligent man ought to do in one: prune it, plant vines in it, dig it.

"I already know what a vineyard's like; it's a labor to labor, father; I'll sweat, I'll have to rest, it's very hot in the summer, it'll make me have callouses on my hands and blisters."

Because of this, you carry your soul about as you carry it, sluggish in praying and giving alms; because of this, your vineyard remains fruitless, without a farm; because of this, it's become a dump and a compost heap; because of this, you think you'll remain without labor? Take it as certain that the greatest labor that can come to a Christian is to not labor, and the greatest disgust and discontent, the greatest torment and fatigue one can have, is this. That one, to obey his flesh, does not want to be chaste, this will be the greatest labor of labors and the greatest torment and pain of torments, and a greater hell than that of the damned, or as great. Question: what is the greatest labor there is? Everyone will say: the one I have. The one who has poverty will say that that is the greatest of evils. Another will say that it's not having children. Another will say that it's dishonor; another, that it's sickness; and others will say that it's many other faults. Let us leave them aside, for they are friends of themselves and passionate for their own flesh.

Let one who is passionless and one of good judgment and reason say it. What is the greatest of the labors that there is in the

---

[56] Sg 7:12.

world?—It is, certainly, to not labor in your soul, in your vineyard; to do evil, to be tepid, to feel that you're not acting as the law of God commands; there is a hell, God died for me, I am obligated to serve Him. The knowledge of him who sees that he is obligated to do this and sees how he does not do it, this is like a woodworm for him who has reason, and like a worm that gnaws his entrails with sorrow. Thus Zechariah calls it *a hundredweight of lead*,[57] because it is a weight that burdens and weighs more than all weights. There's nothing that weighs one down more than having a sin on one's soul, a conscience burdened with remorse and with feeling, so that you say to yourself, seeing yourself lost in sin: "O sinner! You go about wickedly, hell is yours, you've been lost; God has justice, for He will condemn you for what you have done against Him. How can you suffer yourself? How can you fit within yourself? How do you not explode?"

Although this is no more than thinking "God called me to serve Him in this way," in thinking that, according to the diverse talents that God gives men, they are obligated to spend them, barter them, and multiply them in His holy service[58]—if, in this, he feels he's not fulfilling what he's called to, the tepid man, because he does what he ought not, has a great torment within himself. What unrest and disquiet, what nausea the soul bears! What will he do, then, he who acts and goes against what is commanded of him, or stops before doing all of it? If, then, there is labor in sinning and in not knowing how to serve God, stop and think about how you are as you are through not knowing how to labor; think about which will be a greater labor in the service of God: to have a temptation come to you and to conquer it, or to consent to it and suffer what one suffers through having sinned.

You say: "I want to take a rest. Why should I wear myself out by resisting? Doing what my flesh invites me to do seems better to

---

57 Zec 5:7.

58 See Mt 25:14–30.

me than the pain I get from not doing it." Do you know why you deceived yourself? Because you weighed the pain of the temptation against the pleasure of doing your will. Those aren't good balances, nor are you certain of weighing them rightly. You have to weigh pain against pain and pleasure against pleasure. It doesn't go well. Weigh pain against pain, and you'll see which pain is more, and the one that weighs more, toss it out. Weigh the pain that you'll suffer, which is resisting temptation, against the pain you'll suffer if you don't resist, because having offended Our Lord, and see which weighs more. And weigh the pleasure of conquering temptation against the pleasure that delight could give you, if you consent, and you'll find that of conquest much greater, beyond compare, and much happier and more delightful. Setting them side-by-side like this, tossing out the greater pain, choosing the lesser, and of the pleasures, take the greater.

You cannot, brother, be without labor. If you do not labor for God, you'll suffer a thousand discontents, anguishes, and fatigues, changing your thoughts, getting angry at others. There's nothing so changeable as this. A weathervane's not so turnable, nor so fought by the winds, as is he who does not exercise himself in some labor that would fulfill the service and honor of God. If it's a labor that comes, then it thins you out; if a temptation, then it destroys you. He who serves God, then says, no matter what comes to him: "God will be with me, the Lord will help me." What contentment he has! Then he says, "For God, I did what I did; evil, pain, and labor came upon me, but God will send the remedy for it; and, if not, He will be served by whatever happens." In the end, there is nothing that changes him, since, of the two labors, he takes the lesser. You feel labor in not playing, labor in not talking as you're wont to, labor in fasting and praying, in being alone in your house or cell; then I tell you for certain that you'll have a greater labor in the sorrow that the worm of bad conscience will give you and in the contortions it will give you in your heart, seeing what you are obliged to do and what you do not do.

Second Motive: Thinking of Reward

Lord, is there another remedy for laboring, so that we would not be so loose and so lazy? A philosopher boasted that he had found a remedy so to not feel labors. Being asked what [it was, he responded]: "thinking of the prize that they'll give you after having labored by means of the labors and by way of not resting." Certainly, applied to Christianity, this is very good, reasonable, and worthy of being noted and acted upon. This was what made the martyrs pass through such hard torments, and enter, with joy, into the fire and martyrdom, and lose their lives, saying: "This life that I have and lose here will give me another, forever, in heaven; this labor of an hour, which I pass through, will give me a rest that never ends, in the company of God." *They were looking to the rewards.*[59]

Tell me: What difference is there between the man who was good in this world and he who wasn't—when those ears hear God say, "*Call* the *workers* here, on the day of judgment, *and give them their day's pay,*"[60] and when God says, "Let the dead arise in their bodies *and let each be given what he labored for in the other life*"?[61] If you, then, have not worked, nor have been chaste, nor been obedient to God, nor done anything for love of Him, what will you feel when He says, "*Call the workers and pay them,*" and you see that you remain without a day's pay, and that, because of not having labored, you are being sent to the unbearable labors of hell, where you will labor forever? Say it: what pleasure will you feel then, when they tell you that, because of the *jar of water* that you gave,[62] God will say, "Give him his day's pay"? And the day's pay will be the kingdom of God forever, where you will delight with Him and live in rest, without thought of the labor that never comes to you, nor fear that you

---

59 *Aspieciebant in remunerations.* Heb 11:26.
60 Mt 20:8.
61 Mt 16:27.
62 Mk 9:41.

will lose that highest good that has once been given to you. Which will be worth more then, the jar of water, or the sum of money that you left in a chest? Who is he who will not reach for his belt and dress himself for labor and embrace it willingly, since the day's pay that he is to receive in heaven for his labor is so advantageous?

What Matters Is to Labor in Order to Please God

"Lord, what do I have to do? Do I have to go to the wasteland? I'm tired: do I have to thin myself out by fasting? Do I have to give away my whole estate for love of God, so that I have nothing left for my wife and for my children?"

Oh, holy God! Saint Paul says: *If I speak with the tongues of men*, etc.[63] Elsewhere, Christ says that if you give *a jar of cold water* for love of Him,[64] that you will not remain without reward. How, then, are these strings tuned? How will we make this vihuela[65]—which sounds good—harmonize with what they say? Charity does it. *If you do not have charity* with which to love God and neighbor, *nothing avails you at all*;[66] even if you sell yourself in the land of the Moors[67] and give away, for God's sake, the price they gave for you, it avails

63 *Si linguis hominum loquar.* 1 Cor 13:1.

64 Mk 9:41.

65 A type of twelve-stringed instrument popular in Spain in St. John's time, with the shape of a guitar but the tuning of a lute.

66 1 Cor 13:3.

67 "Moor" was a term for a North African Muslim, hailing, roughly, from modern Tunisia, Algeria, or Morocco. There was a long history of wars between southern Europe and North Africa, most famously resulting in the Muslim conquest of much of Spain (renamed Al-Andalus) for centuries. These frequent wars, as well as assaults by pirates, resulted in many Europeans being enslaved in North Africa. Many organizations—most famously the religious order of Mercedarians, founded by St. Peter Nolasco in 1218—were founded in order to raise funds to redeem enslaved Christians. Possibly the "selling oneself in the land of the Moors" that St. John mentions here meant selling oneself into slavery in order to redeem other slaves.

nothing; and *a jar of water that you give with charity* and love *will not go without reward,*[68] if you give it with the intention of serving and pleasing God.

What is "laboring in the vineyard of God"? In the plaza, you can be digging in the field, and another person can be offering God His Son in sacrifice on the altar, and you laboring in the vineyard of God, and the other in that of the devil; that is, if you do it to provide for your children and wife, and the other does it for the stipend or because he wants to seem holy. Hearts are what please God, what God receives, not the matter of the work. So too here, if one does not go about clothed or wrapped up in this intention of serving and loving Him. If you're cane-jousting[69] for the honor of God, and you're going to church in order to see some woman, the places are different, but, because you're at the latter with a wicked heart and at the former with a healthy intention, for you, the church is the vineyard of the demon, and on the other hand, the plaza, the windows, the canes, the bets, and silks are the vineyard of God, when you're working in it.

Let no one deceive himself by saying, "I'm tired, I'm busy; I can't, and I don't have to, and I can't find a place where to listen to the things of God; I have enough to do in providing for my household." Go to the plaza for love of God; love your wife and children for love of God; listen to your Office and an approved tract, making gains

---

68 Mk 9:41.

69 Literally, "playing at canes." This was a game introduced by the Moors of Al-Andalus (see previous note), which involved two contestants on horseback galloping towards each other with sharpened lengths of cane, then throwing the sticks at each other when they drew near, with the goal being to catch the opponents cane and toss it back. I take this description from Joseph R. Svinth's *Kronos: A Chronological History of the Martial Arts and Combative Sports 1350–1699* (2004), at https://ejmas.com/kronos/NewHist1350-1699.htm (accessed August 10, 2023). Confusingly, the same phrase (*jugar a las cañas*) also referred to torturing someone with sharpened sticks of cane, which does not seem to be what St. John intends here.

with which you'll sustain what God has given you as a charge, and take yourself for a day laborer. What God asks is this, a difference in the heart, not a difference in the deed. One and the same work can mean working for God or for the devil, according to the intention with which one does it, because, if you do it with the intention of pleasing God and providing for your neighbor, this is to labor in the vineyard of your soul, rented from God; this is to be His day laborer. He who labors in this manner hopes to receive the day's wage from the father of the household, who is God.

If there were some good laborers, well-lunched in the vineyard, and they were promised that at night, if they had labored well and did good work nonstop during the day, they would be given an abundance of supper and their day's wage, much increased, and they would be well-paid—if they, upon arriving at the vineyard, dropped the hoes from their hands and stopped to play and jump around, to see who could go higher and who farther than the other, and all day long they did nothing but play and laze about and trample the vineyard, at night, when they came, what supper, what day's wage would they merit to be given by the Lord for the day they had thus wasted?

I said: how is your vineyard? Has your soul flourished and shot off vine shoots? Does it have very fresh leaves and very copious bunches of grapes? "Lord, I was sent to dig." And you, what do you think? (Although I believe that there will be someone here who doesn't know why he came into the world, if he was sent to dig or to laze about.) I said: Who created you, now seventy years ago? Did your parents suffice to beget you? There are married folk who don't have children. God created you, because your parents did not suffice to give you the being you have. He ordained that you be born from them in this city, and that you be created in this manner, and that you live in such a house. In all that has happened to you, God took you by the hand and He worked it, not you, nor them. Why did He send you here? To dig in His vineyard. When He says, "Love God with all your might, give alms," that is God sending you to His vineyard so that you might labor on His behalf and in His law. That's what is preached to us every day. We were told, but we abandoned our hoes and played at who could jump higher. Look about those plazas. Doesn't one say, "Is that man rich? I hope I'll go farther; I have to get richer. Do they honor that man? I hope I'll make myself more honored. Does that girl over there have a skirt? I'll get a better one. Does that man have some office? I have measly power, or I'd have a better one." What are you doing all day long? Why aren't you laboring for God? For all of that is just lazing about in order to labor later, without hope of rest.

"Father, we haven't been idle; I'm worn out from labors at home; I go through poverty and sickness, I'm affronted, I live very tired." I know it well, but to be laboring at this is to be idle. "The other day, I had such an estate, and, when I didn't savor it, it was lost to me. The other day, I had such an office, and now they've taken it from me. The other day, I had a good reputation, and they no longer trust me at all." During all the time you're complaining about this, while you're saying that you're more belabored than you are, I tell you, you are being even more idle. Put your hand on your breast: how much of this did you do for God? How much did you bear with patience? In how much of it did you glorify and honor Him? How much did you offend Him? Oh! What liars we are, for we want to deceive God, since you say that you did it for God, and that you say it for God, and, instead, you do it because you can't do more, and for your own interests. Where is that estate that you have? Where is the patience? Where is the love of humility? Where is the memory of God when you did all this? Where did you meet Him in your labors and ask counsel of Him?

Certainly, it is a great shame to see your own blindness, like boys who were sent to their chores, and *instead* were making mud huts and looking at whatever it is that they met on the road, and they forgot why they came and who sent them. Their father says to them: "Kid, where did I send you? What's the answer you're bringing back?

That's the care you took? Where were you? Get up! To pay for your carelessness and tardiness: lashes that pain the boy in his heart." Thus he's paid back for watching the shrews and forgetting what he had to do and who had sent them.

Where did they send you, brother? Where did you go, or to whom? What were you kept and occupied by? This life that you have, what do you think it is? Why did they send you? Wasn't it to work in your vineyard with zealous and timely works? Where's the holiness of your life? Where's the charity you have, that would throw out a scent to make the serpents flee you, so sweet and so comforting? What have you done? Why have you abandoned the hoe you brought for digging and set yourself to playing at who can jump higher? Give alms at that door over there; confess, make your evil known once a year; it's hard to pardon you, like saying it to a stone; sermons annoy you. God give you eyes to see yourself. If you come, what will you say? "I've labored, but I wasn't in the right vineyard."

Spiderwebs they wove for themselves.[70] They labored in vain like spiders, since, for all their labors, however many nights they kept awake, weaving their web, a fly comes and breaks it all and flies right through it. Another wanders around, raving about how he'll rise up, and God says, "What are you weaving?" He wanders around drinking the wind, because they take off their hats and honor him, and [God] says: "What are you weaving?—Spiderwebs." When the fly of death comes and takes you from this life, we'll see what web you made, if it's a spider's or no. Will you not be paid back for the steps you took wandering around, for how you labored in this? Will you not be sharply chastised for how you labored in this way, how you were idle, and will they not ask you for the labor that you were obliged to do?

It was labor to spend the whole night playing without sleeping; it was labor to wander around the plazas in the moonlight and in the

70 *Telas araneae sibi texuerunt.* Is 59:5.

cold and in the serenity of the night, in order to talk to a woman, but spiderwebs were what you schemed and plotted and wove.

Brothers, where are we going? We're walking to heaven. What do you see? What games hold you back? What bird are you looking at? What returning noise? In what vanities do you employ yourself? May that walking turn your heart to God and not to something else, and everything else is stopping and resting, or being idle, or laboring in vain. It is a great evil to be hired for the vineyard, and to leave your hoe. All that time you had for laboring, not for wasting time and playing and laughing and lazing about and playing cards and playing at who's bigger and who's taller.

Third Motive: Seeing the Labors of Christ

The third [motive] that invites us to labor is putting the Lord before us. And He labors so that we might labor. Christ comes into the world and becomes man, and, in being born, He is cold and He cries and spills His blood and walks and sweats, and they seize Him and they beat Him and they crown Him and they nail Him to the Cross. What does Jesus Christ do? He takes some nails in His hands, and, although He took them of His own will, they held Him fixed there, giving Him greatest pains, making Him expend excessive labors. Christ is hung on a Cross, breaking His hands in labor, and you are lazing about, resting and regaling your body; Christ is suffering, and you are viciously delighting in your flesh; Christ is given blows, and you are honored. How can your soul suffer this? You see your Lord lowered to kiss the feet of His disciples, and they come to you with a slave who takes off his hat to another who didn't take his as low as him, and you won't be finished with him, even if they put him on a cross. Ah, sinner! You see your Lord lowered to the dust of the earth, and you want to rise above the air? Being given blows, He is silent, and they're not twenty leagues away from you when you cringe. You see your God despised, and do you not despise yourself for that great excess you see in Him? Can there be a thing that better convinces you to labor than seeing your Lord tired, fatigued, and dying, and suffering a thousand torments and wounds for you?

How Is the Vineyard of the Lord So Ruined?

Oh wicked vineyard! How bold, for he knew what God has done. "Woe is me! For . . ."

"What are You doing, Lord?" *"Woe is me, for I am a man who gleans! I am a man who gathers the clusters that the grape-harvesters left behind."*[71]

"Then what's happening? Why aren't You gathering?"

"There's nothing to eat, not even food that another left behind. I wanted to eat grapes. See how little there is, for I don't even find unripe ones to eat."

"Lord, what are You trying to say, *there is no holy one on earth*?[72] What do You have, Lord?"

"The grapes that I desired are your holy justice, the keeping of My law, not however you want, on the outside [only]; and it is kept for purpose other than I command."

"Why did another harvest the grapes?" In order to fill up his lunacies, his banquets, and jousts, vanities, all that is necessary so that he might act the craziest he can and as abundantly as he wants. They are workers—congratulations!—in the vineyard of the devil, good laborers who will work it very well. Give me the vineyard of God, give me it for an orphan, give me it for a captive, give me it for a mantle for a woman who doesn't have one, so she can go to Mass. They don't know You nor do they care to hear You, and will they do this without punishment? It's a tough thing, to see the overgrowth that's there in the vineyard of the Lord. The vine is full

---

71 *"Vae mihi qui factus sum sicut qui colligit in autumno racemos vendimiae."* Mi 7:1.

72 *Non est sanctus in terra.* Mi 7:2.

of thistles, everything's become a wasteland, without any work, dry, without any watering—what can we do with it?—full of pits and all uprooted.

Solomon had a vineyard. *He handed it over to the guards. They appointed me as guard*, etc.[73] *He handed it over to the guards.* Guards are the vineyard's pontiffs, preachers, priests, rulers, dukes, and counts, marquises, judges. Then what is the vineyard like? One of two things: either the guards do what they ought and the vineyard is as evil as them, so that they do not make use of any of it, however much they labor and keep watch over it, or the guards are laze-abouts and dangerous men, and the vineyard goes well from being ploughed. What happens to the thousands that the pontiff produces for the king or prince? How is such abundance consumed? Where is the multiplication of fruit? What is that great abundance and the peak of power—which he has among his Church and his subordinates during the time that he reigns—going to do? Do we think that the whole office of the prelate is just for getting up here and preaching about how you have to work? There are enough who will tell you that. But there has to be more than this. The prelate has to be so holy, his prayer so powerful before God, that the mother's water will be worth more than the milk that the lady of the house gives. But if we do not know how to importune God or to weep for our faults and for the labors that souls suffer, and so he has no strength for remedies, how much worse than him is the vineyard, dry and lost, without fruit, destroyed, without leaves, without fruit and even without wood, all chopped down and desolate? What's with the guards? The guards of this vineyard—which God entrusted to them—slept, and thieves snuck into it and left not a thing to harvest. The worst of the evils that's in the towns is due to the negligence of the pastors, of the magistrates, and of the clergymen, and of the parish priests, who are careless about the good government and labor that they are obligated to have in their offices.

---

73 *Tradidit eam custodibus . . . Posuerunt me custodem.* Sg 8:11; 1:6.

See how the Gospel noted this: *the men were sleeping.*[74] Through the carelessness of their heads, the vineyard is so ruined that, if the fire of God were in them—which, knowing that there was sin, would break their hearts with sorrow, and they [would not be] consoled until they had repaired it—if this happened, and they repaired it with charity and love, and if they could not do this, with fear and chastisement, another fruit would be given. This being so, we should take up slings and wander about, keeping an eye on the birds and the livestock, so that none should enter into the vineyard. Brother, if you do not labor in the vineyard of God, you have to labor in the vineyard of the devil, for you cannot escape one of the two. Your master and lord, God, is laboring, and you do not want to help Him; aren't you ashamed to see Him laboring, and you abandoning your hoe and sitting down to watch Him as He sweats? Why do you labor with the devil? His prize is his dinner table. Why are you paid with such miserable food, and why are you moved by such an unfortunate day's wage and price?

Be merciful with God, be humble with God, so that you might delight with Him. But if you walk in the works of the devil, you want what you do not want; you will dine with him at night, you will take part in his condemnation and in his torments and in his fires and in the unfortunate life that he is made to suffer in hell.

The Lord of this vineyard is God, and, of the other, the devil. The denarius of this one will be glory, and that of the other, hell. What greater good do you find in serving the demon than [in serving] God? What greater interest do you hope for from hell than from the glory of God? Speak: Why do you prefer to labor with the demon rather than laboring with God? You won't answer me this? What madness is this that you're doing, so confused and so far from good sense! For two lords go out to that plaza to hire laborers, and the one says, "Walk over here, to my vineyard, and I'll abundantly provide for you, and I'll give you gifts, and I'll refresh you, and, at the end

74 *Dormierunt homines.* See Mt 13:25.

of your labor, I'll give you the glory that the blessed have in heaven, in the company of God, seeing Him and delighting in Him"; and the demon says, "Walk over here, to my vineyard, and I'll make you labor, and I'll kill you with hunger and thirst, and, as your day's pay, I'll give you death . . ." What's the reason for going straight after the one who invited you with hell, and turning your back on God, who invites and entices you with heaven, knowing how excessive are the goods that God gives to His own there?

"Don't be astonished if we fall and we're blind and we're deceived. Lord, we are flimsy." Weep and cry out to God and ask Him to show you what you ought to do and to give you the strength to do it, and to make you know that He will help you do it.

Cultivate the Vineyard of Your Soul. Do Not Rest.

What's going on with this vineyard? Certainly you're not saying what the other said: *My vineyard is before my eyes.*[75] Certainly you don't have *your soul before you,* like a mirror into which you gaze. Hold this mirror before you: see what's lacking in your soul; clean it, for it's dirty; take away what harms you, all the rust and gunk that hinder you. Look at yourself.

Take a good plow and turn over the earth and take out the roots, so that the evil can no longer grow, and so that the sun might dry the grass and all the weeds that harm it. Take up the plow, for it's made of wood and iron; take up the Cross, that holiest wood and iron (the nails), set it firm in your soul, so that the evil root might leave, although it pains you greatly. Rip out what's deep in it, what's well-rooted, malevolence and enmity and the desire to win honor from another, although it reaches your soul—the restitution of what belongs to another, which *in another way*[76] takes the defect away—for if you do not rip out the root, later, when the occasion

75 *Vinea mea coram oculis meis est.* Sg 8:12.

76 *Aliter.*

comes, you will fall, since the root of what did you wrong and what hindered your good labor is still green and well-rooted. Now, you walk upon the earth; after death, you will be below the earth, and they will turn you over, as with a plow, from top to bottom and from out to in.

Follow Christ, labor as He labored, hope that He will give you the price of your labors, consider the labor that you're exerting for God here as lazing about, and give it to Him as time well-spent.

"Lord, the vineyard's already turning green again; guard it from frost!" You have begun to serve God; guard yourself from tepidity; don't throw away the devotion given to you, for it scorches and parches it worse than the north-west wind.[77] Guard it from frost, preserve it in heat with prayer, with fasting, with almsgiving, with supplications and importuning to God, with recollection and humiliation. But, ay! Let there be no little worms born on the inner leaves that are the same color as them, for they rot and eat the leaf and make it lose its greenness and freshness that it had before. "Who put this little worm there?" They say it is born from the leaf itself. Doing good works, you have to look out so that there doesn't emerge, from the work itself, someone who will eat it and waste it and consume it away from you. This is the reason why you do this. If it is for your own interest and so that they would consider you good, what danger you have! Whether you rob another or whether you give alms, you do not lack danger; there is danger when you pray and danger when you don't pray, when you fast and when you don't fast.

If you are vain about your good work, a little worm has been born from it, which will make it lose its beauty and freshness, which will make you lose it all. If your crazy little heart says, "I'm already devoted, God already consoles me, He already gives me

---

[77] In Spanish, *cierzo,* describing a specific wind that sometimes blows through the Ebro Valley in northeast Spain in autumn or winter. Interestingly, though it is a very dry wind, which would "parch" a vineyard, it is usually cold, so it wouldn't "scorch" one.

some of His delights, I ought to do something good, it'll be good, since God's already well-pleased with me"; if you already lean on this, you'll lose what is from God. Perhaps the worm is born more from the leaves than from the fruit, from speaking rather than from acting. Keep quiet if you have something good, if you receive some mercy from God; for there is great danger in taking it out in the plaza. Keep doing what you were doing whenever God gives you mercy, shut your mouth, receive the mercies, and know how to please and serve Him.

"Sir, my vineyard already has grapes. What do I have to do until I harvest them, in order to give God their fruit?" See how you haven't labored, and how another bears the fruit away. You did good works for vainglory, for men; others will gather and bear away the fruit of your vineyard. You labored for them if you worked in order to appear good in their eyes. Those who do not labor in the vineyard will not bear away the reward; and those that have, they will delight in their works, and they shall not remain without fruit to satisfy others.

"Then who will suffer these labors, Lord, if they have to spend [their lives] in this toil?" You will go away very well lunched, and they will give you much to eat, and, at night, they will have dinner all set up for you, and all the day they will give you very good company, by which you will be stoked for labor.

"Lord, I cannot labor, for, later, I'll get tired." You haven't lunched, brother. This is the grazing of the glory, of the word of God. Read good books, listen to sermons. Are you thin? Go to the altar. Badly shall it go for him who approaches it without having labored. How many steal this bread, those who go there without sorrow for their sins! To lunch is to listen to the word of God in His holy church; but, if you do not want to eat, putting the food aside, you will die of hunger, and you will grow thin.

"Lord, the company?" If you knew who accompanies you when you labor in good works! Jesus Christ, the Virgin, the angels. With such companions, are you tired? With such aid, are you not happy? Be assured that Jesus Christ was there the whole night *and the whole night He kept vigil in prayer.*[78]

"Lord, how tired I am! And what will dinner be?" So you are the vineyard of God, and God will give you great aid so that you will labor; and, after you are a good vineyard, what will He give you? May you have strength to work for Him, who hired you, and may you approach Him with all your fruit, so that you might attain glory when you leave this life, and so that you might say, "Lord, I come here now, to praise You and to glorify You." No tongue could tell this dinner, *nor understanding understand,*[79] nor reason imagine. Blessed labor, which hopes for such a reward, which awaits such and so good a dinner, here of grace, and later of glory! *To which may He lead us.*[80] Amen.

---

[78] *Et totam noctem pernoctavit in* oration. Lk 6:12.

[79] 1 Cor 2:9.

[80] *Ad quam nos perducat.*

Sermon 9

To Fight Manfully Against the Temptter

(First Sunday of Lent, 2 Cor 6:1–10; Mt 4:1–11)

"Ductus est Iesus in desertum."
"Jesus was led into the desert."[81]

Exordium

WHO *will reveal the face of his clothing?*[82] Our Lord, speaking of the wiles and deceits of the devil, says: Who will uncover the face of his clothing? Who will uncover the face of him who knows so well how to deceive, who finds so many arts and tricks in order to harm us?[83] Few of us can say what the blessed Apostle said, writing to those in Corinth, about a certain sin that one of them had committed: *Are we ignorant about the*

---

[81] Mt 4:1.

[82] *Quis revelabit faciem indumenti eius.* Jb 41:13–14.

[83] I am following the revised word order found in Ricardo García-Villoslada, "Colección de sermones inéditos del Beato Juan de Ávila," *Miscelánea Comillas* VII (1947), 39. The original word order—found in "Colección," 39, n. 2, and in Luis Sala Balust, *Obras completas del Beato Juan de Ávila,* II:173—instead reads, *"Who will uncover the face* of him who knows so much, *of his clothing? Who will uncover the face* in order to deceive, of him who finds so many arts and tricks in order to harm us?"

wiles of Satan?[84] And he tells them to console him who had thus sinned, since he was not dragged into a worse error by the wiles of the demon.

The preacher has to be educated, and the curé, and the confessor: educated and with a degree in this science of knowing the evil deeds and wiles of the demon. Who, then, will destroy them? God Our Lord. And who else? The Virgin Mary, Our Lady, who was always full of grace, and the demon held no dominion at any time over her; for thus her blessed Son said of him: *The prince of this world will come, and he will have nothing in Me.*[85] So the Virgin, Our Lady, could say that he also had no part in her, because she was always pure and a stranger to all sin, and so the pure Jesus Christ departed from those pure innards.

To this Lady, who always used to be and was pure[86] and is full of grace, let us, since we lack it so, commend ourselves, since we cannot say nor hear anything that would be pleasing to God without her favor; and so that she might gain this for us, let us say the *Ave Maria.*

Christ Is Tempted in Order to Console and Advise Us

Jesus was led,[87] etc., *as above.*[88] Today the Holy Gospel shows us a battle that Our Lord had with the demon, how He conquered him, the trick and art that He used on him.

---

[84] *An ignoramus astutias Satanae.* 2 Cor 2:11.

[85] *Veniet princeps huius mundi, et in me non habet quidquam.* Jn 14:30.

[86] Here, St. John uses both of the Spanish verbs for "to be": *estar* and *ser. Estar* more commonly describes a temporary state: *estar* is used to describe how one is feeling, how the weather is, etc. *Ser* usually refers to more permanent characteristics. So St. John first says that she was always in a pure state (*estar,* "used to be"); then he says that she was pure in her essence (*ser,* "was").

[87] *Ductus est Iesus.* Mt 4:1.

[88] *Ubi supra.*

At the beginning of the Holy Gospel, a doubt and question are offered: what was it that moved Christ to want to be tempted by something as low and ugly and filthy as the demon? Even here, a chaste and honest woman is ashamed and is greatly pained by any word that a filthy man dares to say to her, and she is pained, although it is certain that, on her part, there is complete purity, and that she would consent to death before *she would consent* to anything that was against her honor and purity; and this is to be well believed, that, if she could avoid having such a man say any filthy word to her, she would, with good will, avoid it. How, then, did Our Lord, being true God and Truth itself, permit, though being able to avoid it, the demon, who is lies and filthiness itself, to dare to tempt Him and invite Him to an offense against the Majesty of God?

Look through your life for where his speech began, and see how it ended. It began with good and pious words, and ended in, "Adore me!" Like someone saying nothing. Oh wiles and deceits of Satan! Who could avail himself against your arts and against the diversity of temptations with which you assail men? See how it goes, from beginning to end, and from entrance to exit.

Why did the blessed Jesus Christ want to be tempted? What was the reason why, being able to avoid it, He did not avoid it? Some secret is enclosed in this; He wants to tell us something in this; He wants to show us something, since He consented to it. I say that the highest Truth permitted to be tempted for two reasons. The first, Saint Paul says: *We do not have a high priest who could not sympathize with our infirmities, but one tempted through likeness, without sin.*[89] *We do not have a high priest who is not pained by our weaknesses,* [but rather] sympathizing with them, because He has us written in His heart. Jesus Christ does not have a restricted or curtailed love, like us who, if we see our neighbors in some necessity, help them with restrictions, with "yes" to this, and "no" to that, and say, "I already

---

89 *Non habemus pontificem, qui non possit compati infirmitatibus nostris; tentatum autem per similitudinem absque peccato.* Heb 4:15.

did this or that for you the other day; I can't do more now: what's done is enough." Jesus Christ did not act so, but rather helps us and sympathizes with us, not once or twice or thrice, but as many times as we have need of Him; He does not wait for us to call Him, for Him to be invited, and sometimes, tossing this away, He seeks us out, and when we forget Him, He makes us remember.

So great is the love that He has for us in His heart that He never ever forgets us, nor does He take His blessed eyes off our necessities, weaknesses, and miseries, in order to remedy them; nor does He take His favor and hand away, in order to help us and provide for us by means of them, as a true high priest who truly sympathizes with our weaknesses, as Saint Paul says. And, because of this, His mercy consented for the devil, the head of lies and evil, to dare to come to Him and tempt Him, so that, *tempted in everything, through likeness, without sin,*[90] He would learn through experience and know of our temptations, without any sin, because, afterwards, we, coming to be tempted, would console ourselves with having seen our exemplar Jesus Christ tempted, and we would believe that we would be freed by Him as by a high priest who was pained by our temptations, and so that you, brother, being tempted, would not be not dismayed, nor think that you are forgotten by God; instead, you have to believe that, with the aid of the Lord, conquering temptation, it will turn into a crown for you, and its labors and pain into joy.

The second reason that the highest Truth permitted to be tempted is so that you might know, brother, that there are tempting demons and enemies and temptations, and that we always wage a cruel war with the demons, so that we should not be careless.

Tell me: if there were someone right outside, waiting for you, with a sword at the ready, in order to injure you and kill you upon leaving the church, and you did not know this, and, from this pulpit, I advised you of it—"Beware, for they want to kill you right outside; look after yourself"—would there not be a reason to thank whoever gave you this advice?

---

90 *Tentatus per omnia per similitudinem absque peccato.* Heb 4:15.

You'll say: "No, father, for I don't have any enemies; everyone loves me much."

You don't consider them enemies, you don't think that anyone can do you ill, except for him who can take away your honor, or your estate, or your temporal life. I tell you, truly, that there are greater dangers over there, and greater and stronger and more cruel enemies, and that what they want to steal and take away from you is not a temporal and perishing thing but perpetual, that is, [they want] to steal your soul and to make you lose your life, which is God. How many times do you say, *But deliver us from evil!*[91] You pray this devotion, you commend yourself to the Lord, you beseech Him from the heart that He might free you from this evil. Beware, for many are the snares of this, our adversary, and you have great need of the aid of the Lord. Open your eyes, ask Him strongly from the heart, importune Him, *that He might free you* from the evil day *of temptation.*

Certainly, it's a tough thing, the great carelessness we have in this fight, how flimsily we walk about, how little fuss we make about it, and how little fear we have of its cruel and mortal encounters. Certainly, it would seem bad for a soldier to carry merchandise into war, and in a time of battle, to strive after things of peace, and in a time of greater danger, to prepare for strumming and singing and pleasurable things.

We Are at War. The Demon Lays a Thousand Snares for Us.

We're waging a war in that which regards our soul; a war of great importance it is, and a business in which our whole heart ought to be occupied, and an office we have to be carrying out. We don't do this; we're very flimsy, we occupy ourselves with other things that are worth less, we open our hearts so that God would help us in other matters, and we forget this one, though we're so deep in it. This is

91 *Sed libera nos a malo.*

not done well: we're careless, as if there were no war. And what do we lose? We open our door and house; it's a sign that we have little to lose, and we leave it open. What we love greatly and consider great we guard greatly, and we put much security on it, so that we won't lose it. A great sign, and the most certain one, that you have God, is if you greatly fear to lose Him, and if you guard yourself against all the things that could separate you from Him, however great they be.

This one, our tempter and perverse enemy, there's no kind of evil he doesn't intend, nor is there a combat he could give us that he doesn't give. A thousand new arts and inventions he orders and fabricates; a thousand things he feigns, a thousand he conceals; here and there he tempts us; from all sides he assails us, and he never ceases, night and day, in every time and place, to persecute us; and, as Saint Jerome says, *He has a thousand arts of hurting.*[92] And even servants, and great servants, of God, after spending much time in His holy service, find themselves to be new recruits against this warrior, and He arms them with things they don't know how to put their hands around, unless they have the particular aid of our Lord.

The rabble is swallowed up by that, by that which they do not see, without paying heed to it, as Job says: *He will swallow a river, and he will not be seen.*[93] They do not have enough love and care for

---

92 *Habet mille nocendi artes.* See St. Jerome, *Epistle* XIV.4: "You err, brother, you err, if you think there is any Christian who does not suffer persecution, and you are most strongly fought against, if you do not know you are being fought against. Our adversary, like a roaring lion, seeking someone to devour, goes about (1 Pt 5:8), and you think of peace? . . .He pursues me, I say, with hosts, *whose are a thousand names, a thousand arts of hurting,* and do I, unhappy, think myself the victor, while I am taken captive?" (PL 22:349). The phrase St. John highlights is taken from Virgil's *Aeneid,* when Juno is speaking to Alecto, one of the Furies: "You can arm one-souled brothers in battle / and overturn houses in hates; you *can* bring blows / and death-bearing torches on roofs; yours are a thousand names, / a thousand arts of hurting" (VII.335–338).

93 *Absorbebit fluvium et non mirabitur.* Jb 40:18 (Vulgate). Accurately translated, the end of this verse should read "and he will not be amazed" or "he

Our Lord, and for this reason, they do not look enough at these temptations, nor do they guard themselves, with diligence, against the rabid darts of this tempter.

Saint Paul himself says, while advising souls fearful of God and cautious in His service: *Clothe yourselves*, brothers, *with the arms* of faith, *so that you can stand on foot against the ruses of the demon, for your battle is not against flesh*;[94] we have, my brothers, a battle and a fight, and not against just anyone, *not only against blood and flesh, but rather against* some very valiant and forceful enemies, *princes and rulers of this world.*[95] See if there is a reason for us to keep vigil and to guard ourselves with a thousand eyes, having such enemies; and see if it behooves us to separate from the band of the world, which follows its own partiality and has those malign spirits as governors and rulers. Well-ruled will be the republic that has such governors! And unfortunate will be those who live under such a regime; for, although it appears to you that it's going well, if you live in some sin, you're obeying those under whose banner you fight and to whom you are going, in order to be their citizen in hell.

Flee, my brother, from every sin as from hell itself, for hell is that which brings you to hell. How do they not pull out their hair, how do they not weep, how do they not wander about sad and pensive, those who know they are subjects of such tyrants?

The tempter said to Jesus Christ, showing Him all the kingdoms of the world and their glory: *All this is mine.*[96] And the head of lies lied and did not speak truth, because nothing created is his, nor does

---

will not marvel." However, St. John seems to be making a cross-lingual pun here, connecting *non mirabitur* ("he will not be amazed") with *que no mira* ("which they do not see"). To highlight St. John's pun—which is etymologically accurate, as the Spanish verb *mirar* ("to look," "to see") comes from the Latin *mirari,* from the verb *miror* ("to marvel")—I have altered the translation in the text.

94 *Quia non est vobis colluctatio adversus carnem.*

95 Eph 6:12.

96 Mt 4:9.

he have anything in it, nor does he even possess a little ant. What promises he makes, what appearances he puts on for us, so that we would believe him! And he lies in everything. He who is nothing cannot give anything, and if he gives something, it is what he has, which is fire and hell. He invites you to delights; he says that they won't end, that he will raise you to great honors, that he will give you great riches, that he will make you prosper in this life. And he fails in everything, because he has power over nothing, nor can he give anything but what he has, which is to burn in the hellish fires.

What we have said up to now is the least with which he can harm us, because, as these are very clear sins, he can harm[97] no one with them except he who very strongly takes his part, those whom he keeps very busy with the things of this world. The demon wages another war—much crueler and more dangerous, and as much crueler and more dangerous as he does it more secretly—against spiritual persons and times and places, and with arms and things that appear secure, and such is his evilness and cunning that there is no one who can escape his snares.

He will sometimes advise you to fast. A frightful thing, that a demon would say to a servant of God "fast, give alms, be abstinent," and, if you do not do this, he jeers at you and condemns you and he holds you in little esteem, and he goads you and solicits you to be better. And the traitor does all this, not because he gains something from it but rather because he hopes to make you lost in one way or another. He makes you depart from your sins and amend yourself so that, when you are praying for something, you would think that, since you have come so close to God, you are good and holy and pleasing in His eyes, and so that you would fall into a pestilence of pride, by which he will bring you to hell, be it by any path, be it by this or that. Who could count the tricks and ways he has! You'll see that someone is very chaste and that it is difficult to be so; he helps him to be even more chaste and makes him hate women, in order to

[97] A marginal note in the manuscript replaces "harm" with "deceive."

assure him and drive him crazy, seeing himself so high in that virtue. What will I tell you about him? He becomes chaste with the chaste, meek with the meek, all in order to fish some fall from there;[98] as much as he sees some inclined to a certain virtue, so much higher does he raise them in it. He assures them on one side and gives them battle on the other; he feints on one side and wounds on the other, like a good fencer. For this reason, no one ought to be assured in little or in much, in evil nor in what appears good, because, in this, there are great dangers, through the security and appearance of good that he promises us.

"Then, Father, what will I do? How or in what way will I know if the good works that I do and the good words and thoughts that I have are from God or from the demon?"

How? *From their fruits.*[99] Look, brother, when you have worked, or spoken, or thought something good, at how you remained [afterwards]; for if your soul stays a little crazy, if it's stuck on something, if it despises others, if it compares itself to or esteems itself more than others, how clear it is that it is the demon *who gave it.* And when something good has been done, as I have said, and you find your soul empty of humility and crazed and vain in its own estimation, and content, renounce yourself and such goodness, for it proceeds from nowhere else but the demon.

A great piece of advice, which we have to hold to in everything, since our enemy puts snares and traps before us in everything, in order to hunt us. Then, is he not strong? A strongest, hulking beast he is; that giant Goliath—who signifies this, our adversary—challenged the whole people of God,[100] for he leaves nothing unassailed through

98 This is a literal translation of this odd phrase: *para pescar de allí alguna caída.*

99 *Ex frutibus eorum.* Mt 7:16.

100 Per Scripture, Goliath only addresses himself to "the phalanxes of Israel" and "the armies of Israel" (1 Sm 17:8,10); however, it also states that "Saul and *all the Israelite men,* hearing the Philistine's speeches in this way, were stupefied and excessively afraid" (1 Sm 17:11, emphasis added). It is probably from this

cowardice; he assails every kind of person and at every age; he does not leave out the child, however small he be, nor the youth, nor the elderly; finally, he challenges all and assails all, casts his nets for all.

This being so, who sleeps, who eats, who rests, who can be at ease and careless, having such enemies, who do not sleep, nor eat, nor strive for anything else but seeking for a way to deceive us and make us lost? Then, when midnight comes—which is already the hour for the religious to rise for Matins—the demons come, thus solicited, making some not get up and others sleep through the morning. He goes to the official, to the merchant, to the citizen, to see if there is some way he can make him fall. And just as, with the officials, each one gets up in the morning in order to tend to his office, so the demons begin to tend to their own [office], which is to deceive us.

One of them comes and makes you eat a lot, and since he thus grabs on to you, he goes and says to another demon, "Go and tempt that one; see how much he gives in!" That one comes, tempts him with another sin. Another comes and tempts him in another way, and thus the ones are helped and favored and replaced by the others. Another demon makes you not eat much, so that you might break your obedience and go against the will of the prelate, through which, without compare, you lose more than you gain by fasting. And, in this way, he wreaks the damage he wreaks in us, because, on their side, there is a greatest diligence, and on ours, a greatest carelessness and flimsiness. And this being so, as we all know that this is certain, was not that a great mercy which Our Lord did to us in giving us warning, since He willed and permitted to be tempted so that we might look to Him when we ourselves are tempted? Certainly, great was this mercy, and great are the thanks which we ought to always give Our Lord Jesus Christ because of it.

---

verse, and a later one that describes the fear of "all the Israelites" (1 Sm 17:24), that St. John drew the idea that Goliath himself had challenged all of Israel, and not just the armies.

God Aids You. For Your Good, He Permits Temptation.

"Father, I would have liked it more if you hadn't warned me about all this. I would have been good not knowing about that war and the enemies that you told me I have. It would have been better for me if I didn't know this. He's so strong, I'm so weak; I'm careless, and he's so diligent at deceiving me: How can I wage war and endure against so cruel an enemy and so cautious a deceiver?"

God promised His people Israel that He would take them out of Egypt and bring them to a land [that was] abundant in a great way and fertile in all things, and when they were already very close to entering it, they sent certain of the sons of Israel to enter it and look about it and bring back news of it; they were greatly contented with the land and with its freshness, but they came back terrified of its men, for they were very strong, and its cities and walls were also very fortified. When the people saw this, they feared greatly and lost their trust in the promise that the Lord had made them, that He would set them in that land. God was angry and chastised them because they had little confidence in the promise that He had made them.[101]

I have already told you, brother, about your enemies and their cunning tricks and methods; but God is much stronger, in order to free you from everything, and He can do you more good than all the demons can do you evil. God merely wants you to trust in Him, to cast yourself upon Him, to put confidence in Him and no confidence in yourself, and in this way, He will aid you, and with His aid, you will conquer all the hell that comes against you. Do not let yourself fall away from this firm hope because He is angry, or because the demons are many, and many are the temptations, and bold and of many kinds. Be always near Him, because, if you do not have this nearness and strength with the Lord, later, you will fall, and you will fear anything whatsoever. Wholly flimsy and

---

101 See Numbers 13–14 for these events.

fearful, we do not serve the Lord. If we had a manly heart, friendly towards suffering labors for the honor of God, temptations would not frighten us.

How many persons, how many hearts are flimsy and whimpering, because they are tempted, as those thus tempted grow flimsy and discontent, as if God permitted this for their harm! Have patience in your labors and temptations, since it is certain that the Lord permits them for your good. How will God crown your labors without patience? How will God crown you if your own will—which is inclined to avoid suffering—is done in everything? Hope, and bring yourself beneath the shadow of the wings of God, and you will be aided in everything and freed from all evils and dangers. Truly, He loves you and procures your good. He is your Father, and a good father; He aids all, and He does good to those who hope in Him.

"Father, if the Lord has love for me, why does He permit me to be afflicted and mistreated by the demon?" Saint Paul says, *Lest the magnitude of the revelations exalt* me,[102] *so that I do not become proud.*[103] "Why Saint Paul, him being such a friend of God?" This is fitting, so that, in our weaknesses and temptations, we might know the need we have of favor and aid from the Lord, and we might ask Him for favor, seeing clearly that, without His favor and aid, we can do nothing. But temptations and labors have more security than counsels and gifts, because, in grave temptations and labors, you will know that the powerful hand of the Lord is what holds you, so that you will not fall, even though you might still fall into other little temptations of no importance. The reason why you fall in what is little and are not knocked down by what is great and strong is so that you might know that the mercy of the Lord causes you to be on your feet. For this reason, I say that His Majesty consents to God's afflicting you and permitting you to be gravely tempted for

---

[102] *Ne magnitudo revelationum exaltet.*

[103] 2 Cor 12:7.

two reasons, which follow from it: for the glory that you give Him by hoping in Him and giving Him the honor of victory, and also for your own profit, so that you would know your weakness and you keep yourself in humility.

You will see some saintlets[104] who fast and pray and give their alms, not even speaking or murmuring, and because of this, they think that they've done everything. Believe that he who is not tempted cannot sorrow over or sympathize with the tempted, nor does he know how to pray or ask God, nor does he end up knowing Him at all. This is why, when someone who is tempted comes to you, you are frightened, and you jeer at him, and you show him bitterness, because you do not know what kind of thing it is to be tempted, and he who does know, counsels and animates and strengthens him who goes to him, because he is pained for him, and he knows the necessity he has of his counsel. And he who has felt himself tempted will have much better knowledge of how to give himself to God and how to pray than him who has had consolations, because the need for the Lord's hand and favor that he feels will make him humble himself before God and ask Him for mercy upon his labors.

God is not far from the tempted and the afflicted and from those who manfully fight so that they might not be knocked down, for the honor of Jesus Christ, their Captain. If not, look to Saint Anthony, in that battle that he had with the demons, for he said to Jesus Christ, "Where are You, Lord?" And He replies, "I was here, although you did not see Me, in order to crown your victory."[105]

---

104 The Spanish is *santicos,* a diminutive of *santo,* "saint" or "holy one." There is certainly a mocking or sarcastic tone to the word.

105 The reference is to the famous *Life of St. Anthony,* attributed to St. Athanasius; in Ch. IX of the *Life,* after a bitter struggle against demonic temptations, "when [St. Anthony] raised his eyes, he saw the ceiling open up from above, and, the darkness being removed, a ray of light flowing upon him. After the splendor of it, not one demon appeared, and the pain of his body was immediately removed. . . . Anthony understood that the presence of the Lord was

When you see yourself in some need, call upon the Lord, cry out to Him, for He will hear you, for He Himself said: *He will cry out to Me, and I will hear him, etc.*[106] He "cries out" who asks for succor only from the Lord, and from no other creature at all, and hopes for it from Him and not from any other thing. The precious stones with which our crown will be made are temptations and labors; for Saint Gregory says, *However often you resist, so often will you be crowned.*[107]

---

there, and, bringing forth long sighs from the depth of his heart, he spoke to the light which appeared to him, saying, 'Where were You, good Jesus? Where were You? Why were You not there at the beginning, that You might heal my wounds?' And a voice came to him, saying: 'Anthony, I was here, but I waited to see your struggle. But now, since you did not cease to fight manfully, I will always aid you, and I will make your name famous in all the globe.' Having heard these things, arising, strengthened by this, he prayed, so that he might understand that he had, at that moment, received more manly strength than he had lost before" (PL 73:132C–D). *Virium* (from *vis*) typically means "strength" in a more general sense, but, since it come so soon after Jesus says that Anthony fought "manfully" (*viriliter*), it seems likely the author wanted to connote "manliness" (*vir* meaning "man") as well. The word for "manfully" (*varonilmente*), which St. John uses throughout this sermon is a Spanish equivalent to the Latin *viriliter*.

[106] *Clamabit ad me et ego exaudiam eum.* Ps 91:15.

[107] *Quoties resistis, toties coronaberis.* This pithy statement does not seem to be by St. Gregory. The editor of St. John's sermons points to St. Gregory's *Moralia in Job* XIV.XXXV.42 (PL 1062A); St. Gregory doesn't use this wording there, though he does say, "The crown is the prize of victory, which is given from on high so that he who has struggled might be rewarded." The original editor of this sermon—Ricardo García-Villoslada, "Colección de sermones inéditos del Beato Juan de Ávila," *Miscelánea Comillas* VII (1947), 46, n. 14—also points to a passage in St. Gregory's *Homilies on the Gospels* II.XXXV: "In exchange for the labor of patience, the goods of the next world are to be hoped for, so that the prize of our labor begins at that time, when all of our current labor is utterly finished . . . Seek eternal prizes for temporal pains" (PL 76:1265A–B), On the other hand, St. Alphonsus Ligouri quotes St. John's phrase almost exactly (with *coronaris* instead of *coronaberis*), though he attributes it to St. Anthony (*Sermon* XLVII, "On Evil Thoughts"; *Catechetical Instruction to the People* I.VI). Most likely, it is just a pithy proverb, which writers wanted to attribute to a great Father of the Church.

Take up the arms of faith,[108] says Saint Paul; because he who arms himself with living faith, as Saint Paul says here, is strong to resist, because what spiritual and eternal things he has in his heart make him despise all that's right here and to consider little whatever labor comes to him, so that he might attain them.

The [day] of temptation is called "an evil day"[109] because of the labor that the tempted suffers in resisting and because of the great danger there is during the temptation. The great danger is that the devil being so importunate and knowing that some, by not suffering the labor of resisting very long, consent [to him], he gives great importuning, *so that they might, at the least, consent due to tedium,*[110] and because of this, the *day* of temptation is an evil day, since in it, we are on the eve of losing God, if we consent. And although it is true that, on this day, you are in this danger and in this pain, strengthen yourself, brother, with the favor of the Lord, in order to conquer, considering that the pleasure you will have from having conquered is greater than the pain you suffer when you are tempted.

Why is it that a confessor responds to him who recounts some temptation or weakness, "Why did you do that? Why are you like this? Why didn't you do that other thing?", except because he has not been tempted? And, since he has not been, he judges others by himself, and, as there is no man who does not, of his own nature, love or abhor some vice more than another, when he sees in another what he abhors, he cannot—nor does even know how to—suffer it, and he wants everyone to abhor it as he does, and he is terrified lest someone commit it. Finally, because he who is not tempted knows nothing, neither can he console the tempted.

---

108 *Accipite armaturam fidei.* Eph 6:11.

109 Eph 6:13.

110 *Ut saltem taedio consentient.*

What Will We Do in Temptation?

"Father, we're already in this war, and we cannot flee it: tell me, what will we do?"

Let them speak, let the captains speak. Saint Peter says: *Brothers, be sober,* etc.[111] "Brothers," says the prince of the apostles, *be temperate.* He has much reason, certainly. What evils does this eating cause! How many does the enemy knock down! He makes them fill themselves up to the brim, and he goes about laughing at them, and he sends another worse than him, and he says, "What I leave to you! Go and tempt him as you will, for he's good and ready for everything that you want him to do." With this sin, the demon knocked down our first mother Eve, and with this [sin] he tempted Our Lord Jesus Christ today, saying to Him: *Make these stones turn into bread.*[112]

Further, Saint Peter says: *Be vigilant.*[113] We should spend the better part of the night keeping vigil and praying to God to free us from this enemy and to give us strength to cast all evil from us, since our enemy does not sleep, rather, he is always keeping vigil for us, until we reveal a little chink through which he can hurt us and inflict his temptations upon us. And thus Job says of him that he is not content with swallowing the rivers over there, but rather that he hopes to swallow and suck up the river Jordan.[114] He is not content with making careless men fall, but he rather procures and wants to make fall, by his arts, those who are prosperous in the service of Our Lord and who bear His happy and delightful current through the meadows of contemplation and of taste for God and for His sacred Scripture.

---

[111] *Fratres, sobrii.* 1 Pt 5:8.

[112] Mt 4:3.

[113] 1 Pt 5:8.

[114] See the full Vulgate version of Job 40:18, partly quoted above: "Behold, he will swallow a river and not marvel; he has confidence that the Jordan will flow into his mouth." The verse is describing Behemoth. In most versions of Scripture, this verse is Job 40:23 rather than 40:18.

Curates, prelates, look and be vigilant; beware, for the demon knows that the good of others hangs upon you and your example. He labors greatly to knock you down, and he turns the greatest force of his deceits against you, since, by knocking you down, he knocks down many others with you. Doesn't it say over there that *all the force of battle was turned against Saul*?[115] Because, the captain being defeated, he upon whom all have their eyes, they, then, are dismayed. And because of this, the fall of such ones is more striven for and desired by the demon than that of other men, because the latter does not go so far. And you don't have to be frightened or cowardly about waging war against him, since it is certain that the day that you made peace with the Lord, on that same [day], you made war against the devil. If the demon is strong to conquer and deceive you, stronger and wiser is God to defend and aid you. God will aid you more than that one will tempt you.

Roaring, he wanders about, says Saint Peter, *seeking whom to swallow.*[116] *Resist, strong in faith.*[117] Blessed is he who understands this word, and blessed he who, in his heart, has living faith, which keeps him secure among temptations, and strong in labors, secure and meek in the whirlwinds and changes of this age. Keep your memory fixed on and your confidence in the Cross of Jesus Christ, from which the demons flee and go away frightened, and they do not dare to appear before it. Look to Saint Anthony, to what defense he had when amidst all the infernal powers, that is, living faith in Jesus Christ and the Sign of the Cross, from which they went away, fleeing, for they could not stand before it.[118]

---

115 *Totum pondus praelii versum est in Saul.* 1 Sm 31:3.

116 1 Pt 5:8.

117 *Resistite fortes in fide.* 1 Pt 5:9.

118 For instance, see the *Life of St. Anthony*, Ch. XV: "Every one of them disappeared at the first Sign of the Cross" (PL 73:138A); similar episodes can also be found in Ch. XII and Ch. XVIII.

There are some foolish men who, from pure fear, do not dare to go off alone to pray a little. Tell me, what can he[119] do to you? Is not God present there as well as him? What can he do to you in the presence of the Lord, Your helper and guard being there? Go off alone, brother, without fear, and commend yourself to God, pray your devotions, bear living faith, for God goes with you, and He is wherever you are, so neither the demon, nor all of hell, can assail you or do evil against you without His consent.

"Oh Father! How very evil and sinful am I, and he torments me with such evil thoughts, and he makes me believe that God will not pardon me. What shall I do?"

You should trust in Jesus Christ and have living faith which will not forsake you, for the demon does not wander about for any other reason except that of making you despair, aggravating you with your sins, setting them before you so that you would lose faith and hope in the Lord. And so he says, *Raze it unto my foundation*,[120] because this foundation is He who keeps us all on our feet in labors and makes us strong in tribulations, and without Him, we cannot build anything that is good.[121] And by this road and way, the demon enters into temptations in order to knock you down and conquer you, in such a way that, bringing temptations of pride upon you, he might humble you, and, with those of luxury, he might make you more chaste, and with those of wrath, meeker.

"Father, it is very hard, and it torments me." Don't say that; instead, tell the Lord, deep from your heart: "Lord, if Your Majesty is served by my being in this labor and tribulation for a thousand years, which, for my good, you have sent to me, I will be very content with this, and with all that You want to send to me, since I

---

119 That is, the devil.

120 *Exinanite usque ad fundamentum meum.* Ps 137:7. The text here oddly reads "my foundation," though the actual Scriptural text has "its foundation" or "the foundation in it" (*fundamentum in ea*). In the psalm, this is the Edomites's rallying cry for the destruction of Jerusalem.

121 See Ps 127:1.

know that You love me and that You will not send me anything that is not for Your honor and my profit."

King David conquered that great giant Goliath, who had challenged the whole people of God, with stones. So, brother, when the demon breaks your confidence, seek a stone in the sacred Scripture with which you might crack his head and defend yourself against him.

The demon said to Jesus Christ: "Make these stones turn into bread." Christ responds: *Not on bread alone does man live*, etc.[122] Christ meant to say here that *man does not live on bread alone*, but on all that God wills and commands, so that he might live, in such a way that, in order to maintain a man, it is not necessary for him to make bread of stones, but to maintain himself on the stones themselves (*the word in place of the thing*[123]).[124] And, further, he brought Him to the pinnacle of the temple and said: *Throw yourself down from here, for it is written of You that angels will serve You.*[125] Note and learn from Christ's responding to the demon with holy words from the sacred Scripture. You are supposed to read in the holy books at certain unoccupied hours, in order to study it, and in order to exercise yourselves in the words of the Lord, in order to find yourselves attentive in temptations. This isn't done, and therefore, you walk as you walk. He also took Him onto a very high mountain and said: *Adore me, and as much as You see I will give You; all is mine.*[126]

---

122 *Non in solo pane vivit homo.* Mt 4:4.

123 *Verbum pro re.*

124 St. John's point is a little obscure here, but here is a possible interpretation: the stones are the desires and commands of God, which are hard to follow. The devil tempts us to replace the hardness of God's commandments (stones) with soft, easy pleasure (bread). But men do not live on easy pleasure alone; instead, they live on the difficult, yet more rewarding, commands of God. Thus, man should be maintained, not by bread but by the stones themselves, by the hard commands of God, which hard stones will crack the demon's head, as David's stones did Goliath's.

125 Mt 4:6.

126 Mt 4:9.

See how it ended. This is its closing. Christ said to him: *Go back;*[127] *you shall love the Lord and Him alone must you serve.*[128] Confused and put to shame by the responses Christ gave to his temptations, he left, and Christ remained on the field like a strong warrior. *And the angels came to serve Him.*[129] Does this not remind you of what Melchizedek did when Abraham had won that battle? He offered bread and wine.[130]

Be strong, brother, during the time you are in this world, in fighting manfully against the demons and their traps. And if you act thusly, not only will the angels come to serve and console you, but Jesus Christ Himself will come, and console you, and strengthen and embrace you, and give you grace for this conquering, and later, His glory, *to which may He lead us.*[131]

---

127 *Vade retro.* Most manuscripts of the Vulgate have Christ's response here as simply "Go, Satan" (*Vade Satanas*), but some have "Go back" (*Vade retro*) or "Go behind Me" (*Vade retro me*). These additions are probably inspired by Christ's similar words to St. Peter, "Get behind Me, Satan"—*Vade retro me Satanas* (Mk 8:33) or *Vade post me Satanas* (Mt 16:23).

128 Mt 4:10.

129 Mt 4:11.

130 See Gn 14:18.

131 *Ad quam nos perducat.*

Sermon 10

Let Us Conquer God in Prayer

(Thursday of the First Week of Lent, Ez 48:1–9; Mt 15:21–28)

"Miserere mei, fili David; filia mea male a daemonio vexatur."
"Have mercy on me, Son of David; my daughter is illy vexed by the demon."[132]

Exordium

SO that the Lord may send us His grace, and so that all that we say may be unto His glory and praise, let us supplicate the glorious Virgin Mary to gain this for us, and so that she would do this, let us say, *Ave Maria.*

Christ Departs, Conquered in Joust and Tourney with the Canaanite Woman

Have mercy on me, etc.[133] The words that will give our sermon its foundation were said by an afflicted woman to Our Lord Jesus Christ, and she gained what she asked of Him. Saint Matthew writes them, chapter 15. It seemed good to me to preach about her, because this woman has great devotion. These words say, in our tongue, "Jesus, son of David, have mercy on me!"

132 Mt 15:22.

133 *Miserere mei.* Mt 15:22.

Among the things of God there are pastimes, just as there are, too, among the things of the world. We see in the Gospel that was chanted last Sunday a joust that occurred between Christ and the demon, and how Our Lord Jesus departed it a conqueror. Today, we will see another [joust], in which He will depart conquered. Powerful and strong are the arms which conquer God. It was the demon, last Sunday, who was tempting Christ, and he was conquered by the words of the Sacred Scripture. Today, a little woman, and a stranger, came to the field, to make battle,[134] and she bore a rude suit,[135] and she took to words with Christ, and she conquered Him and made Him say: *Woman, great is your faith; what you will shall be done.*[136] Is this not a good joust? Is this not a good tourney? What a good war, where the woman conquers and makes what she asks for be done!

This history of the Canaanite woman is very well-known; all of you know it; but what you did not understand the first time, it is impossible for you to not understand, after hearing it another time; for this is the condition of the Sacred Scripture, that, in one and the same step, the more one rises to a greater perfection of life and knowledge of God, the more does one understand what was not understood before. The sacred Scripture of God does not grow old; we always find, in what we have read many times, new things to understand and secrets that we had not understood at other times. And for this reason, let us tell the holy Gospel now.

The Pharisees were very great fasters, and they made a huge show about the outside parts of holiness, and one day they asked Christ why He did not make His disciples fast. And Our Lord rebuked them and called them hypocrites, because they did not take as much

[134] There is a pun here in Spanish: the phrase "to make battle" is literally "to make field" (*hacer campo*), since *campo* can mean both "field" and "battlefield."

[135] *Pleito* refers to a legal suit or complaint; *ruin* can mean "vile" or "despicable," or, less harshly, "ill-mannered" or "low-brow." The phrase is found in a modern-day quip among lawyers: *en pleito ruin, palabras sin fin [in a plea poorly-penned, words without end].*

[136] Mt 15:28.

care for the things within as they did for those without, which could be bad and good. Having done this, *He went away from there to Tyre and Sidon,*[137] cities of Gentiles, of infidel people, Christ making us to understand, in this going away, that He went away from the feigned hearts of doubled[138] men, who held to and cared for nothing more than keeping up with good appearances. He went away from there, from those who had damaged hearts.

The Christian's principal care must be for his heart. May God keep us from having a damaged and sick heart! Just as, in what is bodily, sickness of the heart is a great evil, so it is a much greater *evil* to have a damaged heart in what is spiritual. The Lord goes away from there, and a woman goes out to the road, since she had a demoniac daughter. If you curse your children and give them to the demon, why do you marvel that he takes them away? Is it a big thing for him to take what you give him? So, he would even want to take you yourselves, if it were possible for him. A searing of fire upon such a tongue, which commends the creatures of God to the demon! Don't do it, for the love of God! Keep yourselves from commending your children to the demon, or to a creature equal to the demon, for it is very wild company, that of the demon, and very much so.

She goes out to the road. She had heard very good things said of Christ, and how He had done great miracles and cast out the demons. She went out to Him on the road. Blessed is he to whose ears have come this news of Christ! We have to give a reward[139] to him who brings it to us. In saying what Saint John said—*Behold the Lamb of God*[140]—his disciples go after Him. Is it little news to say that you have Someone who loves your soul so much, who holds

---

137 Mt 15:21.

138 Recall St. James's rebuke of the "double-hearted" or "double-souled" man (Jas 1:8), which inspired Søren Kierkegaard's flinty sermon, which often goes by the name *Purity of the Heart Is to Will One Thing.*

139 *Albricias* specifically refers to a gift given to the first person who brings someone notice of some good news.

140 *Ecce agnus Dei.* Jn 1:29.

you so piercingly in His heart, that He died for you on a Cross? Rewards! For He has come who will make friendship between God and men, who will make God meek, who will give you joy in your heart and will console you in your labors!

This is He who has rescued you from the power of the demon and from the subjection of sins, and who took evils and labors away from you, and filled you up with all goods and rests. What will we do, having heard such joyful news, except go after Him? How sadness and pain flee, and hope grows, having heard the news of the Gospel! When you understand the power of the Gospel and receive its promises within you, when you receive it, when you work this faith in you, a blessed good and support and hope has come to you, which will take away all your evils, weaknesses, and disconsolations, and a power and strength that takes away every adversity and dismay away from you. And when it is not seated with firmness in your heart, even when the ears of the body have heard the Gospel, you do not have its force and promise working in you.

Good Arms Are: Faith, Mercy, and Perseverance

This foreign woman heard with the ears of the soul, and with this faith, she went out to the road to ask for remedy for her labors. Listen! Perhaps this happened you at some point. You had some need; you asked the Lord with faith; look to this experience, if God let you know that, although He delays, He would give you what you had asked for, and that He would answer you. You'll sometimes feel, when He delays, an I-know-not-what, an I-don't-know-how-this-is-so; when we ask with faith, we are made to know that we will be heard and that we will be given what we asked for; you feel, sometimes, that your petition was effective. Look at this well. The prophet David says: *Blessed be the Lord, Who did not separate my prayer and my mercy from me!*[141] If you pray to the Lord with faith, says Saint James, *He will not take His mercy away from you.*[142] Prayer and mercy are inseparable companions. Prayer of the heart, which flows from living faith, will attain what it asks for. If the Lord has done mercy to you in giving you the gift of prayer, He will also give you what you ask for, because, even if He delays in *giving* it to you, He does not forget it.

This woman went out well-armed, and said aloud: "Jesus, *son of David, have mercy on me!*"[143] She's not sick; how is she saying, Have mercy on me? It's as much the ill[144] of another that pains her as her own. To take another's ills as one's own, to suffer with[145] them as if we suffered them—we don't understand this word. Who is there now who feels the affront and the need that his neighbor suffers, who is pained by his ills as if he himself suffered them, and who feels himself poor with the poor, and tempted with the tempted, and afflicted with the afflicted? We don't know what that's like. We don't understand this language. "Rather, Father, sometimes I can console myself with another's ills, with how many more they have than I do."

---

141 *Benedictus Dominus qui non amovit orationem meam et misericordiam suam a me.* Ps 66:20.

142 *Securus esto quoniam non amovebit misericordiam suam.* This quote is not by St. James; the closest Scriptural quote is from 2 Maccabees 6:16: "Because of this, He will, indeed, never remove His mercy from us; though chastising *them* in adversities, He will not abandon His people."

143 Mt 15:22.

144 Literally, "evil" (*mal*), but, in this case, it refers to the "evils" one suffers—pains and troubles and misfortunes and sufferings—rather than the evil acts one commits. In the following paragraphs, one should keep in mind that every instance of "evil" or "ill" is the same Spanish word (*mal*).

145 This is the literal meaning of "sympathize" and its Spanish equivalent (*compadecer,* from *con,* "with," and *padecer,* "to suffer"), which St. John is emphasizing here. "Compassion" has similar roots, though in Latin (*com* or *cum* means "with," and *passio* means "suffering," as in the Passion of Christ).

A bad sign is it, very much so, to not feel another's ills; to not feel what others suffer is evil. Saint Paul preached to those of Corinth: *If one member suffers something, all the others suffer with* and are pained for him.[146] Thus you have to be pained for your neighbor, for he is a member and companion of where you are. As, when your toenail is sick, all of your body is pained, so when your neighbor is in some pain or need, feel it, since you're both in one body. It is a great evil for one member to not feel the ill of another; it is a sign that he is dry, since he does not feel or have life to feel the ills and labors of another member.

And this is the rule of charity, that we do not know where it dwells.[147] What the flesh does through kinship, will grace not do through charity and the Holy Spirit? If we do not have it, let us ask for it from the Lord. This good Canaanite woman says this. She says it to the priestly fathers. Thus she calls to you, sad ones, since you carry so much on your backs. When they want to ordain some people, they examine if they know how to chant and read, if they have a good patrimony; so that, if they know a few canons and have a good patrimony, (woosh!) they're ordained. What will God examine them about? About charity for all and about prayer, if they know how to pray well and to importune God for their neighbors and to render Him meek and to make friendship between God and men, and to feel another's ills and weep for them, and to feel what they do not know and what they do not see. And if he does not know this, what does all the other stuff profit him? This we learn from the Canaanite woman.

Who is there here who does not have some little share in the demon? You're frightened at what I'm saying. Later on, I'll tell you something about this.

---

146 *Si quid patitur unum membrum, compatiuntur omnia.* 1 Cor 12:26.

147 What St. John seems to mean in this sentence is that, when we have charity, we feel our neighbor's pain so deeply that we can't tell where it originates, in us or in our neighbor: through charity, we feel the pain of all equally, since we are all one body.

Here, He kept silent towards this woman, and last Sunday, He spoke with the demon, when the words of the sacred Scripture conquered him. Have you suffered a lance-wound in prayer, when you left it as cold and as dry and as devotionless as you entered it, and sometimes worse, and harder? Learn from this woman, who went to plead God, and since He did not answer her, she went to His saints, betook herself to His holy disciples, and pleaded them to speak for her to Jesus Christ. What solicitude she brought from the ones to the others! And how she importuned them, so that the apostles said to Christ: *Do it already*, Lord, *what this woman begs of you, since she's coming, shouting after us.*[148] And Christ said: *I am sent only to the sheep who were lost from the house of Israel.*[149] Now You answer with this, Lord, after being importuned and pleaded by her and by the holy apostles, whom she made pleaders? With this, You go away? This is worse, Lord, than keeping silent. Who would suffer this *even* for a Milanese harness?[150]

You put yourself in a little corner in order to beg something from God, and it seems that He throws you away and says to you: "Walk away, shut up, leave it alone, this isn't for you, it can't happen, you won't be saved, you're not good with God, go off over there." And the woman argued with all of this. She goes to Christ and says: *Lord, help me.*[151] You're not even wounded, and you're asking for help? What treats are you coming to ask for? Where there's more disfavor, is there greater hope?

Abraham believed in hope against all hope.[152]

---

148 *Dimitte illam, quia clamat post nos.* Mt 15:23.

149 Mt 15:24.

150 The armorsmiths of Milan, particularly the Missaglia family, were considered among the best armorsmiths in Europe. The harness was the central portion of a suit of armor, consisting of front and back plates attached with leather straps; sometimes it only covered the torso, while, other times, it covered the thighs as well.

151 *Domine, adjuva me.* Mt 15:25.

152 *Abraham in spem contra spem credidit.* Rom 4:18.

"Father, why did Our Lord will it that our faith be so high, above all our judgment and understanding? For what reason does He make us believe things that surpass our human nature and knowing? Since God thus willed it, for what reason does the blessed Saint Paul tell us that we should be *prepared to give a reason for our faith to whoever asks it of us*?"[153]

Understand it in this way: that you don't have to give a reason for the things you believe, for what God commands you to believe, but you have to give one for the way in which you believe it. He tells us that, beneath the sacramental species, there is the most Holy Body of Our Lord Jesus Christ; there's no reason why you should believe this, but there is a reason, and a very great reason, why you believe it in this way. And so with all the other articles.

There is no doctrine that has as much reason to be believed and has less rationale in human nature and in the rules of it. The sect of Mahomet[154] had some false miracles; these were not enough to be a reason why it should be accepted. The law of Moses had miracles, but, after Moses's passing, did they come? They saw no miracle, but rather they believed in those they heard tell God had worked among their ancestors, in their time; so some received [the law] of Moses because they saw the few miracles that had been done; others, because they heard tell from their fathers what had been done. Why do you not accept this, when God has done so many and such great [miracles], and in varied places, in order to confirm it? How many dead have arisen, sick been healed, blind enlightened, and a thousand thousands of things that could not be recounted in a lot of time! Thus said King David: *Your testimonies have been made excessively believable;*[155] *Your testimonies*, etc. Then, why did the Lord order that we should believe something contrary to reason? Why, seeking God, does it seem that He draws away from us?

---

153 1 Pt 3:15.

154 A version of the name *Mohammad* that was frequently used throughout the Christian world.

155 *Testimonia tua credibilia facta sunt nimis.* Ps 93:5.

Abraham believed in hope against hope.[156] His age said to him: "You're already old, and your woman too; how could you beget or have a son?" Read Theophylact about what *Paul* says: *I was not infirm in faith.*[157] He says: "It takes more labor to believe well than to work well, and it takes more soul and strength to believe than to work."[158]

He wanted us to not ask for signs, as I preached to you on Sunday.[159] So the Canaanite woman does this: Christ having cast her away, she returns, as at the first, with fresh forces. And see what response is given her. Jesus Christ does that, not because He is cruel and bitter but rather so that the whole world would know this woman's greatest faith. *It is not good to take the bread of the children and give it to the dogs.*[160] "What you ask for is for children, and you are a dog." Beware, Lord, for, if she is a dog, perhaps she will bite you.

He says to you: "She who has done this asks for mercy? She who has sinned so much dares to approach God?" This is to call you a dog.

"*Even so, Lord!*[161] I do not ask for what is given to good children. You've given so much to the children, You've preached to

---

156 Rom 4:18.

157 *Non fui infirmatus in fide.* Rom 4:19.

158 See Theophylact of Bulgaria, *Explanation of the Letter to the Romans,* on Romans 4:19–21: "He, then, 'not being weak in faith,' but having mighty *faith,* did not look upon his own body, already deadened with age, nor upon the double death of Sarah's womb (for it had died both from old age and from sterility), nor 'did he hesitate,' that is, he did not doubt at all, nor waver, 'but he was strengthened by faith.' See, then, how he shows that the believer needs much power. For many have disparaged faith as a painless thing, but they magnified works as being sweaty and demanding power. It is therefore necessary, he says, that the believer be of great and powerful soul, so that he might drive away the thoughts of unbelief, just as, therefore, Abraham, too, was strengthened by faith" (PG 124:398C–D). Obviously, St. John has heavily paraphrased Theophylact's comment.

159 St. John probably meant to say "yesterday": the Gospel for Wednesday of the First Week of Lent includes the verse, "An evil and adulterous generation seeks a sign, and a sign will not be given it" (Mt 12:39).

160 Mt 15:26.

161 *Etiam, Domine.* Mt 15:27.

them, taught them; You were born among them, You healed, resurrected—what is there, Lord, that You haven't done for them? *Give to me out of what remains.*"[162] The perseverance and living faith of this woman seemed good to Him, and He answered her: "*Woman, great is your faith; may what you ask for be done;" and her daughter was healed from that hour.*[163] Enough! For the Lord goes away conquered, since all that the Canaanite woman asked Him for, with great faith, had been done.

For Many Things, Prayer Is Good. Let Us Pray Always.

You've seen this joust. Let's go and enter into the war. Who is there who does not have a demoniac daughter? It seems like we pull out our hair when we say or hear that the demon dwells in someone. What is it for God to dwell in someone? What is it for the demon to dwell in another? For God to dwell in someone is to have the condition of God, and for the demon to dwell in someone is to have the condition of the demon.

The sacred Scripture calls someone fox, lion, goat, wolf, and likewise other names, because that one has a condition like that of that animal whose name he bears. If you feel something of the demon in your heart—although you don't have mortal sin, you'll have a bit of wrath, eating a bit too much, sometimes sleeping more than is needed—such a thing will torment you like a demon; and that other thing, which is to have him in the body, is due to sins or because, sometimes, Our Lord permits it him to possess the body as he possesses the soul, because this is the penalty of sin, that he who possesses and torments the soul would possess and torment the body. In the primitive Church, those who were thus possessed by the demon were allowed to stay until it was time for

162 Mt 15:27.
163 Mt 15:28.

the consecration, and when [the priests] were about to consecrate, [the demoniacs] went outside.[164]

The greatest strength is needed in order to not be possessed by the devil, because, beyond his temptations being great and powerful, the worst thing about him is his being importunate. Some there are who have left themselves be conquered by his importunity alone. Other times, there are other demoniacs in regards to the body, and it is not a penalty of sin, but rather because God wills and permits it for some good for the man.

A very holy monk begged the Lord that He would permit a demon to enter into his body, so that the people who came to see him as a saint, seeing that he was a demoniac, would take him for evil and a sinner, and thus, their visits would cease, as well as the fear he had of losing God, seeing himself so esteemed by the people. There are few of these. On the contrary, I know that there is someone who would become a demoniac so that they would take him for a saint.

When Saint Paul asked that temptation be taken from him, wherever it came from—the demon, the flesh, other men—the answer came to him: "Suffer the slaps of the demon, because he does not possess your soul." The demon is wise and strong enough that we should always walk about, beard over shoulder, keeping watch, armed, so that we don't miss one little buckle, so that he doesn't wound us through it, because he always wanders about, seeking an opportunity to kill us. There is no greater force and arms against

---

[164] In the early Church, the division of the Liturgy of the Word and the Liturgy of the Eucharist had consequences, as those who were not fully in communion with the Church—catechumens, demoniacs, public penitents, etc.—were forced to leave the church during the Liturgy of the Eucharist. Hence, another set of names for the two parts of the Mass is "Liturgy of the Catechumens" and "Liturgy of the Faithful." A remnant of this practice is found in the Byzantine Divine Liturgy, where, just before the Creed, which precedes the Eucharistic Prayer, the priest cries out "The doors, the doors"—that is, "close the doors to keep out those who are not in full communion."

him than Confession and Communion. Commune, confess, and you will be strong for this battle, and meanwhile, fight much stronger. Let's set this aside, since we'll never finish with it, and what we said about this battle last Sunday is enough.

Who does not have a tiny bit of wrath? There are some temptations that come from the demon, and others that come from ourselves. And if you want to know when they are from us or when they are from the demon, look, when you are tempted, at if they assail you most valiantly. When they do not come so robustly nor with that much impetus, they are from ourselves. Just as when, in order to do a good work, you hide yourself and do it with a fervor like fire, you say that such a one comes from God, so, on the other hand, when you do good works with little fire, you know that they have come from you, since they do not go forth with ardor, as the others went forth. Saint Paul says to the Thessalonians: *You have received the word, not as spoken by men, but rather as truly God's, He Who works with efficacy in you who have believed.*[165]

Who is there who does not have something of the demon, even if he does not understand it? If what walks about in your soul is God, so that you would ask God, the Gospel recommends prayer to us today. "Lord, and are those arms enough to conquer temptations, and to make the demon flee, and to give the soul strength?" Read, and you will see how often prayer is recommended in the holy Scripture. Jesus Christ prayed in order to take and choose His holy apostles.[166] Who knew the things that He had to do better than Jesus Christ? And He prayed more and better than anyone. He did not work in this world without raising His eyes to the Eternal Father and praying. Pray, brother, since you have such need, and we have to pray. Pray before eating, pray before going where you have to go; don't do anything without first commending it to God, since it matters so much whether we go aright or we err.

---

165 *Accepistis illud non ut verbum hominis, sed sicut est vere verbum Dei, qui operatur in nobis.* 1 Thes 2:13.

166 See Lk 6:12–16.

Christ says: *It behooves to always pray and to never fall away.*[167] *We always have to pray*, night and day and in every place. It is a good style and manner of speaking, when we commend something that ought to be done with diligence and caution and many times; as when we want to say that someone eats a lot, we instead say, "he does nothing but eat, his office is none but this." Thus here Christ says that we should always pray; He means to say that we should do it many times and with care. And, since it is very important to us, let us not labor "hands on the distaff and eyes on the door,"[168] as they say of the wicked woman.

Jeremiah says: *Let us raise our hands and heart.*[169] Let not your hands hinder you from commending yourself to God. You will perform gracious and very pleasing prayer if, wherever you find yourselves, you raise your hearts to God and keep Him present in your memory. Who will hinder you from doing this?

"Lord, show me what I have to do so that I don't err." God has no closed door. Always, night and day, you can enter to do business with Him, very profitably. And He will hear you and console you and do all that is needed, all that would be to your profit. A great mercy it is to have that Lord so close at hand, with whom we do so much and such important business. It behooves [us], then, to always pray and to always be before Him. And whatever thing you think of, be it already woven and done, do not, because of that, be careless in calling upon the Lord, so that His aid and favor would come, without which that business you're thinking of is neither begun, nor mediated, nor brought to a good end. Do not think that you can do any good thing without His counsel; rather, without Him, you will err in everything.

Joshua came and, by not commending himself to God and receiving answer from Him, he was deceived by the Gibeonites,

---

167 *Oportet semper orare et numquam deficere.* Lk 18:1.

168 A Spanish proverb to describe someone who's not paying attention to the work at hand.

169 *Levemus manus et corda.* Lam 3:41.

who came with ripped cloaks and ripped clothes and stale bread.[170] And this is why, however lettered and highly commended you be, you should commend it to God, and place it in His hands, and do not trust in yourselves nor in your own brain nor understanding, and trust in God, and you will not err. And if you have erred, it is because you trusted in someone who could not be certain, and this is no fault of God's.

"Father, I'm already considering this well, and I'm considering it again, and I'm thinking about it, and I'm talking it over with my friends, and I've commended it [to them], so that they would consider it." This is lacking, because you do not commend it to God. And even if Our Lord revealed to you that He would save you, or some other thing, you shouldn't grow tepid or leave off pleading Him because of this, just as if He had not made you certain about it. Read *ad Romanos, ["to the Romans"]* 1:5; Saint Paul says: *But I know that, coming to you, I will come in the abundance of the blessing of the Gospel of Christ.*[171] And later he tells them that they should plead to God much *for him, so that He would free him from the hands of the infidels that are in Judea.*[172]

Origen says that, in order that the order God has given for the execution of *His* ends not be impeded, it behooves us to pray and commend ourselves to Our Lord, in what we know and in what we do not know, and in what we understand, and in everything whatsoever that comes into our hands, since in everything, we need and lack the counsel and favor of God.[173] And if you ask me "why do we walk about like this?" I'll tell you, "Because we do not pray, because we have forgotten prayer, and we don't even know what kind of

---

170 Jo 9:3–5.

171 *Scio autem quod veniens ad vos, in abundantia benedictionis Evangelii Christi veniam.*

172 Rom 15:30–31.

173 See Origen, *Commentary on the Epistle to the Romans* X.15: "Although he said above, *For I know that, coming to you, I will come in the abundance of the blessing of the Gospel of Christ,* yet, even though he did not yet clearly know what was to come, he knew that prayer was necessary." (PG 14:1276B).

a thing prayer is, and we carry about weak, dismayed, fear-filled, unconfident souls, without yoke or gift." That is to say: whatever ills we have come through a lack of prayer, and you lose many goods because you do not know how to communicate with God.

You are filthy and dishonest, and you see that He is chaste and honest, and you are ashamed to speak with Him, since it seems to you that He knows your evil, and you are ashamed of doing some evil thing before Him, and you flee from thinking about it. If you were to accustom yourselves to putting yourselves before Him, if you were to communicate with Him a while, you would not last very long in sin, because His purity and holiness would cause you to be ashamed of returning to such holy conversation while wrapped up in sins. Communicate with Him, meet alone with Him for a little while, in your little corner, if you want to be healed of your ills. If, each night, you make an account before Him of how you sinned, in speech and deed, during the day, when you go to give this account on another day, you will, from shame, have at least stopped doing many things that you had done and have labored to amend yourselves. And this is why those who give an account with God cannot for very long, nor even for a little while, endure in their sin and offense; but he who does not take up this rein and guard, nor comes before the light and clarity and purity and holiness of God Our Lord, spends months and years without amending himself— and God forbid it not be for his whole life![174]

Although It Might Seem the Opposite, God Always Awaits Our Prayer

"Lord, why isn't it being given to me?" Because He wants something for you that is more befitting. If God delays [in giving] what you ask Him for, all the better and more befitting your salvation. God

174 This practice resembles the Ignatian Examen, and it could be influenced by the Jesuit practice. In his later life, St. John fervently encouraged his followers to join the Jesuits, who were similar to a community he had envisioned creating.

is not deaf nor rigorous; He loves you, He wants your good. Our Master and Redeemer Jesus Christ said: *I give You thanks,* Lord, *because You* always *hear Me.*[175] In these words, He also gave thanks on our behalf, for we are always heard by God, *You Who save those hoping in You.*[176] Let us hope, let our hearts trust in the Lord, let us not fall later if, later, He does not answer us, for He will answer us, and He will give us what we ask Him for, for did He not boldly say, *Ask, and you will receive,* etc.?[177] Why would the highest Truth have said this, if afterwards, He was to be deaf to our petitions and to our labors and hide Himself when we call upon Him? He will not fail to answer, even if He delays a little, and if He delays, do not be distressed, for thus it behooves, thus is it needful; have strength to hope in Him with faith, for He will fulfill His word and answer us, since He has said to us that we should seek and we should ask and we should call. Oh shame of men, that they do not come, being invited and called!

"Then, why isn't what I ask for being given to me?" Because it's not befitting. "Why doesn't God give me children? Why does He give me illnesses? Why does He take away my goods? Why doesn't He give me this? Why doesn't He give me that?"

Because, if you are good, you'll be content with this, and if not, it befits you, because you are evil. The good Christian asks only for that which does him good, that which brings him to heaven. God says: "Then let Me do it, for I will give you what best befits you for the end you seek." That is, *for those loving God, everything cooperates unto good.*[178] Never ask something of Our Lord without leaving that bosom bare: *Deum ["God"].* Oh, if this were so, that door open, that condition clear! Lord, give it to me, if it would fulfill my soul.

---

175 Jn 11:41.

176 *Qui salvos facis sperantes in te.* Ps 17:7.

177 *Petite et accepietis.* Jn 16:24.

178 *Diligentibus Deum omnia cooperantur in bonum.* Rom 8:28.

Saint Augustine says that *the angry God grants many things which the kindly one would not grant.*[179] You are sick; you ask the doctor to give you water or something else that He knows will hurt you.[180] He says: "It's not befitting; beware, because it's dangerous." You importuned Him, and you said to Him that He denies you what you ask Him for because He wills ill for you. So many times you ask Him to give it you and say: "Take it over there, drown yourself in it." Never urge Him, but rather say: "Lord, if Your Majesty wills to fulfill me, give this to me, and if not, don't give it to me, if it would not be for my salvation;" and in this way, you will always go aright, and the Lord will give you only that with which your soul will be saved, and be content with that, since, if you are good, this must be your desire, and this must be your end in all your demands. If He does not give you what you ask for now, it is through the great love that He has for you, and because He knows that, giving it to you, you would be lost. And if the doctor does not give you what you ask for, it is so that he would not do you the ill it would do, and not because he wills ill for you. And for this reason, you shouldn't complain because you

---

179 *Multa concedit Deus iratus, quae non concederet propitious.* See St. Augustine, *Sermon* 354.7: "Sometimes the angry God gives what you ask for, and the kindly God denies what you ask for. Truly, when you ask from Him things which God praises, which God commands, which God promises in a future age, ask securely, and lean into prayer, as much as you can, so that you might receive. For those things are granted by the kindly God; those things are lavished not by His wrath, but by His mercy. But when you ask for temporal things, when you ask with measure, when you ask with fear, trust Him that, if they are profitable, He will give them; if He knows they will hinder, He will not give them. But what hinders or what profits, the doctor knows, not the sick man" (PL 39:1567).

180 The Fathers loved the example of dropsy: the disease, so they said, caused excessive, unquenchable thirst, but, if given water, the patient would get sicker or even die. As here, it was used as an image of how we can be driven to desire things that would actually hurt us. Today, the term "dropsy" has been replaced by "edema," an excessive swelling in parts of the body; one of the common causes of edema is congestive heart failure, one of whose symptoms is excessive thirst.

don't have something, since what seems to be un-love comes from greater love; and granting what He seems to be denying you would hurt you, although it seems the opposite to you; and He answers you, although it seems that He has become deaf.

To others, God does not give what they ask, so that, at the time of payment, they would receive a greater reward. It is clear that the wage of ten days is worth more than that of one. All that you labor for and afflict yourself for now, Our Lord will reward you with the justly demanded wage for it, and if, later, He does not pay it, it is for your greater good. There is another principal reason why what you ask for is not given you. You *are* given to. You do not ask without being given to, because to not give to you *is* to give to you. Tell me, if there was a man in greatest danger, because they wanted to slit his throat, and this man asked for a locket—man, beg them not to kill you, beg them to pardon you, ignore the locket right now! Your soul is in some sin: isn't it worth more for you to be given what would better fulfill you, so that you might enter into your soul and say, "Why does the Lord deny me this? I must have done something against Him; I've made Him angry, since He doesn't want to hear me"? This is a great spur, and it is very worthwhile for those who are careless and stuck in some sins.

"Lord, I asked for this, You don't answer me; You don't show me Your face; it grieves me that You're so bad to me; I'll amend myself, Lord. Pardon me! I want to be better and to do penance." In this way, by denying you your demand, you will know your sins, and you will fear the rigorous and fearful face of God in the other world. Now, a sin is a fearful thing. Since here, in this world, where things are not known as they are, the rigorous justice of God causes such fear, how will *a sin* seem there, where it will be clear in its weight and ugliness? How will it be to appear there, before God, laden with sins and offenses against Him?

You complain that "God doesn't hear me, He doesn't console me, He doesn't give me devotion; I feel Him to be rigorous, it seems like

He's dismissing me, I find contentment in nothing, I don't know what He's doing to me." Brother, look at this very well; be wary of what Our Lord God does many times with those who treat their neighbors unlovingly. Think well if you have angered some neighbor, if you are rude to those you deal with, if you are pained over what they suffer, if you love them or if you mistreat them, because *in the way that you have dealt with them, in the same way our Lord will deal with you*;[181] make use of this in order to deal with your neighbors as you would want and desire God to deal with you; those who give an account to God give their souls a mirror, as it were, and in that same way, they converse with and treat their neighbors as they want and desire God to treat them. Then know that there is no surer barter nor one that matches so surely as treating your neighbors well and lovingly and doing them all the good that you can, because thus will the Lord deal with you.

Do you see how, if you were later given what you asked for, you wouldn't gain as many goods as you were given to know by being denied it? Beg that you might hold this *in your hands.*[182] *He who closes his ears to the needs that he sees and hears the poor suffer*, will become needy and *will cry out* and will ask for aid, *and he will not be heard.*[183] A just judgment, for, since you do not hear the cries and anguishes of the others who suffer, God will not hear you yourself when you are in need.

"Lord, why don't You hear me?" *He who closes his ear lest he hear the law.*[184] Look, too, at how, when we speak to you on behalf of God, and we tell you that this will fulfill you, even though it hurts you, *the preacher* tells you, "God tells you this," and he makes no more imprint on your heart than if no one had told it to you. God

---

181 See Mt 7:2; see also Mk 4:24.

182 *Per minibus.*

183 *Qui obturat aurem suam ad clamorem pauperis, clamabit et non exaudietur.* Prv 21:13.

184 *Qui obturat aurem suam ne audiat legem.* This line is based off of a phrase from Isaiah 33:15: "he who closes his ears lest he hear bloodshed."

sent it to be said to His people by the prophet Zechariah, chapter 7: *Judge a true judgment; make mercy and mercies, each one with his brother; neither widow, nor orphan, nor stranger, nor poor man, shall you deceive.*[185] And they did not want to do this, they hardened their hearts and stuffed up their eyes so to not understand him; because of which, God was most grievously angered, and He told them that they would thus cry out, and He would not hear them.[186]

A great evil is it to not feel this, that we call upon God and He does not want to hear us. We have to do mercy towards our neighbors, love them, succor them, so that, when we call upon God, He will hear us. And if, sometimes, He does not answer so quickly and shows Himself bitter towards us, it will be for our greater good and warning. Since this is so, let us call upon Him, and if He does not answer one time, let us call upon Him again and again, for He will answer us and gives us grace and, later, glory, *which may Christ Jesus, Mary's son, deign to bestow upon me and you, He Who lives and reigns with the Father and Spirit, God through all ages of ages. Amen.*[187]

---

185 *Iudicium verum iudicate, et misericordiam et miserationes facite unusquisque cum fratre suo, et viduam et advenam et pauperem et pupillum nolite calumniare.* Zec 7:9–10.

186 Zec 7:13.

187 *Quam mihi et vobis praestare dignetur Christus Iesus, Mariae filius, qui cum Patre et Spiritu vivit et regnat, Deus per omnia saeculorum saecula.*

Part 2

“Celebrate His Suffering with Joy”

Sermon 16

The Life of Christ, a Pilgrimage

(Easter Monday, Acts 10:37–43; Lk 24:13–35)

"Peregrinus tu solus in Hierusalem?"
"Are you alone a pilgrim in Jerusalem?"[188]

Exordium

I CAN'T give you the letter of the Gospel today first, as usual; it depends upon others, which I have to declare in the course of the sermon. Therefore, you'll have to pardon me for now, since I think I'll pay it back with interest. For all, grace is necessary.

Jesus Christ Takes on the Disguise of a Wanderer

Something that caused me a great admiration is recounted to us in the Gospel. He appeared to His disciples in the figure of a pilgrim or a wanderer.[189] In Latin, not only a pilgrim, but a

[188] Lk 24:18.

[189] St. John's two words here are *romero* and *peregrino. Romero* specifically refers to a pilgrim on a pilgrimage to Rome, though it is often used to mean "pilgrim" in a more general sense. *Peregrino* is the more general term for "pilgrim," but it can also mean "wanderer" or "foreigner," which connotations St. John seems to intend here. Throughout this sermon, I have generally translated both words as *pilgrim,* except when they are used right next to each other, as here.

traveler.[190] It's already taken up in that term. In it, I want to treat this step that I proposed. Thus I think the evangelist—one of those who came to Jerusalem to celebrate the feast—used it.

I say, then, that it is a thing of admiration and fear for me, to hear that Christ disguises Himself, that He takes on the mask of a pilgrim. If a knight, a prince, a king disguises himself, they do not cause fright because they do it many times, to pass the time, to enjoy some feasts. God, who does not do anything suddenly and without forethought, who disposes all things in wisdom[191]—who will say that He disguises Himself and takes on another persona? And further: even if He wanted to disguise Himself, what is this? He did not take on the disguise of a knight, of a king, of an emperor, of a consul, of a high priest, of a prophet, but rather He takes the mask of a pilgrim.

In this, it is necessary that we take as a firmest presupposition, as a very certain thing, that this was not without a great mystery, since all of His works have one in themselves. Therefore, the diligence we take in discovering it will not be superfluous or wasted.

So you would understand in one word what I thought to say and declare in many, I say that He took it on because of this, because, in everything, His life strangely agrees with that of a pilgrim. The whole life of Christ was nothing else but a pilgrimage, a wandering, as Bernard says,[192] the end, etc. We could see this, if we want, in

---

[190] St. John is emphasizing that the Latin word used in Luke 24:18, *peregrinus,* can mean a foreigner or a traveler, and not simply a pilgrim in particular. *Peregrinus* is the source of the Spanish *peregrino,* "pilgrim," which St. John sometimes uses alongside *romero.*

[191] This phrase recalls a number of verses, such as "How many are Your works, O Lord: all in wisdom You have made" (Ps 104:24) and "You have disposed all things in measure and number and weight" (Ws 11:20). We might also recall the description of Wisdom as the one who "disposes all things sweetly" (Ws 8:1).

[192] One of St. Bernard of Clairvaux's Lenten sermons (*Sermon* 7, PL 183:183C–186A) is entitled, "On the Pilgrim, Dead and Crucified," but the focus is on the Christian's life as a pilgrimage rather than Christ's.

that *saying* of the prophet: *Like a pilgrim in the land, and a traveler turning towards lodging.*[193]

He was, in everything, like a stranger and pilgrim, a traveling man. This seems clearer if we consider the things that concurred in Christ, in His life and death, for this purpose. What particularity makes a pilgrim? In what does he differ from other men; why [is he] unknown?

The first [particularity] I find in the habit. He dresses in a crude cloth, which can better withstand the storms of the sky; he has a cape of thick cloth, and along with this, that wrap themselves in leather in order to better defend themselves against the water, and so that, in this poor habit, they might not be recognized in the lands through which they have to pass.[194]

The Word, equal with the Father, wanted to make a pilgrimage and to pass through the world as a pilgrim. He puts on clothes of thick cloth, the sackcloth of our humanity; He passes by, unknown, with this clothing, and He was so, *lest they recognize* Him, etc.,[195] in order to receive, in it, the waters and storms of torments that they were to unleash upon Him; that rain of lashes and hail of pains, flood of blows and wounds, injuries, that whole whirlwind unleashed upon that clothing of His humanity. It stopped there, for it could not reach what was within; the soul was in quietest glory and rest, because, in the holocaust of the patriarch Abram, the ram's throat was slit, but Isaac was safe and saved, which was a sketch of that other [sacrifice].

Second, he is known *to be* in poverty. They do not have their own houses. Today they are in one inn or hospital, tomorrow in another;

---

193 *Quasi peregrinus in terra, et viator declinans ad manendum.* Jer 14:8.

194 Confusingly, St John switches from a singular to a plural subject in the middle of the sentence. The verb *encuerar* is typically used in the same sense as the idiom "to leave someone in leathers" (*dejar en cueros*), meaning to strip someone bare or leave someone destitute. Here, though, it seems St. John is using the term in its literal meaning, "to en-leather."

195 *Nisi cognovissent.* 1 Cor 2:8.

they are in a foreign land, beyond their nature. In this, we well find Him a pilgrim.

He says of Himself: *Foxes [have] dens*, etc.[196] He had no income, house, nor possession. Saint Mary received Him as poor, and others helped Him with His household, He being the Lord of all the [households] of the world, though He is born in another's house, though, on the day of His death, they buried Him in another's shroud and another's sepulcher, and they celebrated His funeral.

"How? Great God, are You not Lord of all that is created? How do You lack what is needed?"

"Because here I am a pilgrim: *My kingdom is not*, etc.,[197] to be persecuted. Up there, in heaven, in that life which is forever, I will reign in glory and eternal rest."

Christ Goes as a Pilgrim to the Cross, to Suffer

This pilgrim—so I find in Scripture—made three pilgrimages or trips on His journey, three, all to Jerusalem: First, *from the womb,*[198] to suffer; second, from the Cross to Jerusalem, to give life to His body; [third], to the other, the supreme [Jerusalem] of glory.

Where does our Jesus go on pilgrimage? To Jerusalem. He always acted so that we would understand how all of His traveling was towards Jerusalem. *There all will be consummated.*[199] There He will end His journey. "Where are You going?" To visit the temple of Solomon, a devotion to see the Ark of the Covenant, to offer sacrifice, *Holy of Holies*?[200] No, none of this. In the bosom of the Father He was *from eternity.*[201] He does not lack this. One thing remains for Him: the holy wood of the Cross. He goes on pilgrimage. This is the temple and the

196 *Vulpes foveas.* Mt 8:20.

197 *Regnum meum non est.* Jn 18:36.

198 *Ab utero.*

199 *Ibi consummabuntur omnia.* Lk 18:31.

200 *Sancta Sanctorum.*

201 *Ab eterno.*

ark, *Sancta Sanctorum*, where Christ, the High Priest, has to enter to offer incense *because of sins.*[202] He comes on pilgrimage to offer His soul, Father and body, mother, life and blood for sinners.

Just as men hang their statues in the temples they have visited, He wanted to follow this rite in a strange way, being a pilgrim to the Cross. He was not content to leave His statue of wax, but His statue of Himself, a body hung, nailed on the Cross. And as they are wont to carry back insignia from their pilgrimages, in testimony of having walked them, like those who come from Santiago laden with scallop shells,[203] with jet from Montserrat,[204] with certain images from Guadalupe,[205] Christ took those scallop shells, the precious wounds: His feet, hands, and side remained signed. "*See that I am*[206] the pilgrim. I come from there. You see the signs." And the Father in heaven, and the apostles on earth, and the wicked in the judgment, shall always remember such a meritorious pilgrimage.

Without sin, and so painful a pilgrimage. He had made a forceful vow to fulfill a promise to the patriarchs and prophets, giving them the word and even the license of His Name. They pleaded for it: *Remember Your word.*[207] *The Lord swore truth to David*, etc.[208] And He had obedience to and a mandate from the Father. *As He*

---

202 *Propter peccata.*

203 Scallop shells are a traditional pilgrim insignia, especially for pilgrims who visit the shrine of St. James (Santiago) in Compostela, after traveling the path simply known as "The Road" (*El Camino*).

204 The Santa María monastery on the mountain of Montserrat in Catalonia is renowned for its ancient statue of the "Black Madonna." In honor of its distinctive color, it seems pilgrims would buy rosaries and other items made of jet as mementos.

205 This is a reference to the Guadalupe in Extremadura, in Spain, not Guadalupe in Mexico, though the appearances of Our Lady of Guadalupe did occur during St. John's lifetime. The Spanish Guadalupe has a "Black Madonna" like Montserrat.

206 *Videte quia ego sum.* Lk 24:39.

207 *Memor esto verbi tui.* Ps 119:49.

208 *Iuravit Dominus David veritatem.* Ps 132:11.

gave a mandate to Me, so do I do.[209] He had a command; He could do nothing else. If it frightens you that He, being God, had [a command], though He could in no way sin, that He did His part, although He was free, His not being able to go against Him[210] does not hinder Him from being able to have *a command.* Being free was enough to fulfill it. He is one predestined; He cannot not save Himself, and because of this, He has a command—although free—to save Himself.

What was the cause of this vow? How strange a devotion! Men make vows, seeing themselves in labors, in torments; God being in His glory, what does it matter if He vows or obliges Himself? So painful a thing He did not do for Himself, for He had no need. Fathers, when they die without being able to fulfill or satisfy [a vow], leave their legacy to their sons, so that they might fulfill it. Adam could not make satisfaction for his sin; already knowing, in [Adam's] dream, that God would be made man and [Adam's] son, [Adam] left [Jesus] this burden, so that [Jesus] would satisfy [Adam's] testament.

Alone a pilgrim. A great crowd of them, after the loss of the seat of paradise. A strange singularity in Christ, regarding His pilgrimage, that He rests on the throne and is walking, *traveler, attainer*;[211] He suffered on the Cross and delighted in glory. Alone amidst all His labors, *in the end, the disciples fled,*[212] for His greater pain. He lamented on the Cross: *Why have You abandoned* Me?[213] "*Respice*:[214] Look upon Me hung here, beaten; look upon this, My sacrifice, which I offer You for men; look upon Your Son."

---

209 *Sicut mandatum dedit mihi, sic facio.* Jn 14:31.

210 That is, the Father.

211 *Viator, comprehensor.*

212 *Ultimo discipuli fugerunt.* Mt 26:56.

213 *Ut quid dereliquisti?* Mk 15:34.

214 On the Cross, Jesus quotes the first verse of Psalm 22, which begins, in the Vulgate: "God, my God, look upon me: why have You abandoned me?" St. John continues referencing this psalm in the next paragraph.

In You the fathers hoped.[215] All of them He helped. Martyrs, with the meditation on the better part. *I am a worm.*[216] And David for Him: *I will look to the right.*[217] All those whom He healed and cured, who shouted for Him as king, disappeared. There was no one who returned for Him. And thus on the day of His labor He says: *The winepress I have trodden alone.*[218]

Journey to the Sepulcher, to Arise

Second journey: To give life to the body. It is a fearful thing that Christ made pilgrimage to hell. It's not evil, if you know how to do it. Not few are the pardons, the indulgences that are gained by drawing souls out of pain. It has to be done in life; in death, it is dangerous, you'll stay there if you spend the night. *Vide* Guevara: *To hell alive.*[219]

Inasmuch as he has life, he goes down to hell with consideration, considering the pains, which he fears and which separate him from sin. And it is so necessary, as you say of the *pilgrimage* to Santiago. He who does not do this in life knows that he has to travel the *milky*

215 *In Te speraverunt* patres. Ps 22:4.

216 *Ego sum vermis.* Ps 22:6.

217 *Considerabam ad dexteram.* Ps 142:4.

218 *Torcular calcavi solus.* Is 63:3.

219 *Infernum viventes.* See Antonio de Guevara, *Epistolas familiares* (Madrid: Matheo de Espinosa y Arteaga, 1668), 96: "For the unfortunate one, who once spends the night in hell, will always remain buried there. He who dawns in glory will never see the night, and he who spends the night in hell will never see day, because the chosen have day without night there, and the damned will have night without day. . . . Let us now descend to hell through contemplation, so that we will not later descend through eternal damnation. Let us descend to it by fear, so that they will not drag us there by the scruff of our neck. Let us descend to it by steps, so that they will not later drag us there by force. Let us descend in the day, so that they won't drag us there at night. . . . It is a very holy thing to descend to hell in life, so that we will not descend there later in death." This letter is a commentary on Psalm 55:15: "Let them descend to hell alive" *[Descendant in infernum viventes].*

way[220] in death. Try to enter into hell with your consideration; with his will, he does not expect his steps to go badly. As Christ does it in death, for this reason, He is called "alone a pilgrim," alone among the dead, free to not stay there, the only one who does not go to be captive, to snatch them out, *a spirit going and returning*,[221] to be lord of the demons.

Augustine divinely recounts the fear of those infernal spirits[222] as they saw Him so powerful, so resplendent, with that standard of the Cross before Him, fearful, stunned: *Who is this?*[223] Away from Him, they entered into some subterranean caverns, fleeing from the glory and splendor of Christ.

He arrives at the gates where those holy fathers were detained in dark and shadowy prisons. Aloud: "*Open, princes* of death, to the *King of glory*, since He leaves those of the fault destroyed. Open, for

---

220 *Via lactea.* It is an ancient tradition that one way to find the pilgrimage path to Santiago de Compostela is by following the Milky Way, the "path of the stars" (*iter stellarum*) in the night sky. For instance, Book IV of the twelfth-century *Codex Calixtinus* describes Charlemagne noticing this: "And then he saw, in the sky, a road of stars that began in the Frisian Sea and, extending between Germany and Italy, between Gaul and Aquitaine, passed directly through Gascony, Wasconia, Navarre, and Spain, unto Galicia, where, at that time, the body of Santiago lay hidden, unknown." See María Pilar Perla Mateo, "Santiago, un camino escrito en el cielo," *Heraldo*, July 25, 2021, at https://www.heraldo.es/noticias/sociedad/2021/07/25/santiago-un-camino-escrito-en-el-cielo-via-lactea-1508375.html (accessed November 21, 2023).

221 *Vadens spiritus et rediens.* Ps 78:39.

222 See Pseudo-Augustine, *Sermon* 160.2: "And when, like some splendid and terrible pillager, He reached the end of the shadows, the impious and Tartarean legions, beholding Him, terrified and trembling, began to inquire, saying, 'Who is this terrible one, and blazing with snowy splendor? Never has our Tartarus received such a one, never has the world sent such a one into our cavern. He is an invader, not a debtor; He is an tax enforcer, not a beggar; we see a judge, not a supplicant. He comes to command, not succumb; to rip out, not remain . . .'" (PL 39:2060). The demons' terrified speech goes on in this vein for quite some time.

223 *Quis iste?* Ps 24:8.

it is just that He rob the demon's field, since He leaves it conquered; that He sack death, since He killed it; that He grab spoils, like a valorous captain, skillful in arms." They fall. The King enters, and He brings great clarity along with Himself. Consider the press of those ancient saints, prophets, women, elders, in coming to kiss the feet of the Redeemer. Feel the great joy of their hearts, the thanks they give Him: "You have come, Redeemer so called, so hoped for and desired, called for years and centuries—how we have hoped for You! Immense thanks we give You, since You have not forgotten us. You have remembered Your own, Lord, since You had the piety to remember to visit us; do not forget us when You go from here: bring us with You!"

After consoling that multitude of souls, the Redeemer of the world waves the banner of the Cross. After Him, that multitude of captives singing praises, with the great delight they feel in seeing themselves departing from there. It remains to be seen where that holy squadron, having departed from those parts, having come into the world, stopped. I believe that, on that journey, they paused for a bit, I don't think it was an hour. About where He was with them, nothing certain can be known. The saints conjecture some things; as for me, it seems more[224] certain and reasonable to me that He stopped in the earthly

224 St. John originally wrote "more," but later wrote in "very" instead. Ricardo García-Villoslada, the editor of this sermon, thinks this change relates to an issue brought up when St. John was questioned by the Inquisition. It had been reported to the Inquisitors that, when explaining St. Augustine's interpretation of a Scriptural passage, St. John had said, "I could give another, better explanation, but, by my being, I don't want to say it." St. John replied that he didn't remember saying that, but, if he had said something similar, he would instead have said, "I could give another, good explanation, but, by my being, I don't want to say it." See Camilo M. Abad, "El proceso de la inquisición contra el Beato Juan de Ávila: estudio crítcio a la luz de documentos desconocidos," *Miscelánea Comillas* VI (1946), 116. The note referencing this questioning is found in Ricardo García-Villoslada, "Colección de sermones inéditos del Beato Juan de Ávila," *Miscelánea Comillas* VII (1947), 289, n. 25.

paradise, and so I understand that verse: *Today in paradise.*[225] There He was on Friday and Saturday, until Sunday at dawn.

A blessed saint contemplates here: those fathers, desirous to see His body, begged Him to take it up again. The patriarchs: *Arise, Lord, unto Your rest.*[226] The ark, the humanity where the divinity was enclosed like a treasure for our rescue, with which You made payment in the bank of the Cross. The Kings: *Arise, Lord, let them be scattered,*[227] the guards of the sepulcher; let them flee, since they hear the thunder. *Prophetae ["Prophets"]: Arise, judge Your cause.*[228] Abraham: "Beware, lest Your Name end up destroyed; the apostles waver; You are obliged to make Your word truth." Eve and the others: "*Arise unto my judgment*;[229] these complaints and stones are for me; all cast the fault on me, they sue over my transgressions; be a voice for me; make the world understand that, if I brought death, from me came He who brought life; let the Virgin advocate for me in her prayer."

Don't be careless: *Arise, my glory; arise, psalter and zither; I shall arise the dawn.*[230] At dawn's laughing, that blessed soul departs from paradise to the sepulcher; He dresses in His body, to which He communicated His glory, as brocade; thus He departs. The angels roll back the stone; the guards are frightened, stunned with great fear and surprise.

Pilgrimage to the Heavenly Jerusalem

Third journey: to the Jerusalem on high. For forty days He detained Himself in the world to confirm the faith in His disciples and to attend to matters touching the foundation and increase of His Church.

---

225 Lk 23:43.

226 *Exsurge, Domine, in requiem tuum.* Ps 132:8.

227 *Exsurge, Deus, dissipentur.* Ps 68:1.

228 *Exurge, iudica causam tuum.* Ps 74:22.

229 *Exurge iudico meo.* Ps 35:23.

230 *Exurge, gloria mea; exurge psalterium et cithara; exurgam diluculo.* Ps 57:8.

Primo die [On the first day], five stations. To the Virgin, to visit and console her for the immense sorrow that she had felt. We do not have this from the Gospels, but we do have it from the saints. Ambrose, *Liber de virginitate [Book on Virginity]*.[231] The reason which convinces one that it is true is what Christ said: *Qui diligit me, diligetur a Patre [He who loves me is loved by the Father]* (Jn 14:21). *Ad eum veniemus. Cur non? Ego diligentes me diligo [Let us go to Him. Why not? I love those loving Me]*. Those who loved most He consoled first, the women more than the apostles, and the Virgin even more.

I believe that Saint Gabriel first entered to give the news, to ask for the reward.[232] Kneeling: "*Queen of Heaven!*[233] Later, He will be here with all the cavalry of the prophets." Him having scarcely finished, Christ enters. The Virgin, occupied with recollection, pauses, and doesn't move. She kisses those wounds full of splendor and glory. "Oh most holy body, which I saw so beaten! You are as delightful to me now as you were painful then, bruised. Now I see my pain consoled." Eve arrives: "Blessed are you! Through you, life; through me, death; all will be free through you."

He leaves her with them.[234] He goes to the Magdalene. She did not want to leave, and she saw Him; so going, all together saw Him. They went to report Him to the others. This being so, Saint Peter saw Him. He came. He confirmed their news. Those of Emmaus had already left. He appears to them. It doesn't say what He told them. It's conjectured that He told them: "The dream of Adam is understood in regards to Christ *et Ecclesia ["and the Church"]*."

---

231 See St. Ambrose, *On Virginity* III.14: "Thus Mary saw the resurrection of the Lord, and she first saw and believed. Mary Magdalene saw too, although, up to then, she had wavered" (PL 16:270A).

232 *Albricias,* the reward given to the first one to report a piece of good news.

233 *Regina Caeli!*

234 Beginning here, the recorded sermon gets choppier and choppier and devolves into a sketch. It seems St. John never got around to giving the end of this sermon a full written treatment.

Moses asked God to show him His face. *My back parts you will see; set up on a rock.*[235] Moses closed his eyes. Thus the glory of God passed by, which he saw from the back. *A people closed of eye until Christ passes by; after the resurrection, His glory is to be seen.*[236] *Moses, sent into the water by his mother,*[237] the daughter of Pharaoh takes him out. *Christ, tossed out into torment by the Synagogue, is received by the Gentiles.*[238]

Sampson, with the gates on his shoulders, departed from the city; surrounded by his enemies, or, *better, our faults,*[239] which had closed off heaven, [Jesus] departed from the world. That of Jonah: the whale swallowed him live. Joseph, imprisoned with the cupbearer and the baker, departed from there with his honor, a companion with him.

"Mane Nobiscum, Domine."[240]

Thus He appears to Christians. They receive Him in order to throw Him out tomorrow, while He wants them to cry out: "*Remain with us, Lord;*[241] don't pass on so; stay with us." The Gospel of industry: how we shall detain Him, so that He will not go away. If you are a rich knight, you compel Him in the poor; if of the Church, you speak of Him with you; later, you will hear Him speak, not as a pilgrim.

"Don't come to leave us later. We won't receive You just to throw You out tomorrow, with offenses. Detain Yourself by grace." If you want God to hear this, take up this doctrine, drawn from the Gospel.

Three states: *ecclesiastics*: A business of speaking of and dealing with Him, turning over the Gospel and Scripture, meditating,

---

235 *Posteriora videbis; posui supra petram.* Ex 33:23.

236 *Populus clausus oculis donec Christus transiret, post resurrectionem visurus gloriam ejus.*

237 *Moyses, a matre in aquam missus.*

238 *Christus a Synagoga projectus in tormentum, a gentilitate suscipitur.*

239 *Melius, culpis nostris.*

240 *"Remain with us, Lord."* Lk 24:29.

241 *"Mane nobiscum, Domine."* Lk 24:29.

teaching. He will not pass on. Because they speak of Him, He has become their brother. *The knights*, powerful to compel Him, where are they? See those poor; force them, as the disciples did Christ. You have to be importunate, since you are the ones who receive mercy in giving to the poor. *This is the way*[242] by which they go to heaven: *The pasture of the rich is the poor.*[243] A great cross, to suffer their importuning. He never wants His confessors to command them to fast nor to pray, but rather to bleed their purses. This is their cure; they are never saved except through this. *The commonfolk*: in peace with their neighbors, let them do no one evil. In conformity, they will have Christ.

Being together, Christ appeared to them. To give Him glory.

---

242 *Haec est via.* Is 30:21.

243 *Pascua divitium pauperes.* Sir 13:19.

Sermon 37
Processions of Passion and Procession of Joy

(Vigil of Corpus Christi)

"Pro eo quod laboravit, anima eius videbit et saturabitur."
"Because of this, that he labored, his soul shall see and be satisfied."[244]

Excellent Singularity of the Feast of Corpus Christi

THE most just reasons for why this holy festivity of the Body of Jesus Christ Our Lord was instituted and celebrated in our Christian Church, in recognition of and thanksgiving for this ineffable mercy that the loving Lord did to us, through wanting to stay with us here—He Himself, through the real presence in this Most Holy Sacrament—we have noted them in other sermons. And what it particularly behooves us to treat of at the present is of an excellent singularity that this feast has that, thus, by being worthy of much consideration, such as is not present in any of the other feasts, however great they be, it causes much admiration and gives one a desire to know its cause.

Instituting the day of this holy feast, and [ordering] that it is a [day] of rest and that its own office is prayed and that it has solemn octaves, was a new thing in the Church,. because it was newly instituted by

[244] Is 53:11.

Pope Urban IV and confirmed by the holy Council of Vienna, as we have said in another sermon.[245] But if we see that there are also, in the Catholic Church, many other feasts, of the Lord as well as of His saints, which are celebrated alongside all those which are called "solemnities," this [feast] does not seem to have any singularity or advantage over the others, since we do not see how it exceeds them.

It is true that he who looks with attention on the splendor of this sacrosanct mystery, in which the very person of Jesus Christ Our Lord is present, and with whom we celebrate the feast, will find that this feast truly shines some lights and places a feeling in the soul, so that, although there is similarity between this and the others in celebrating with solemnity, there yet appears a particular excellency, and uncommon majesty, in this one. And he who wants to well prepare himself for receiving what is given in it will feel what a particular thing the feast of Corpus Christi is; and he will see fulfilled in himself what is written of it: *You have provided for the poor, Lord, in Your sweetness.*[246] But, although this is so, and though this is quite enough of a reason to esteem this holy feast, what causes a singular marvel in it is the Church commanding us to hold a procession tomorrow with as great a solemnity as our strength can afford, and to take the Lord out of His royal palace and carry Him through our streets with sweet songs, feasts, and great jubilation. This so precious particularity is not performed on any feast, either of the Lord or of His saints, although it is [performed] on the happy days of His birth, resurrection, and ascension, in which, with singular delight and most just cause, the heavens and earth rejoice.

And if this departure of the Lord was in order to visit and commune some sick man, although this is a thing worthy of great admiration and something which demands a singular thanksgiving for so loving a mercy, yet it is not new in the Church, nor is its cause very hidden; for it is certain that that charity which made Him depart from heaven to

---

245 St. John's *Sermon* 35 describes the institution of Corpus Christi in detail.

246 Ps 68:10.

Bethlehem and, later, to the Cross, to save sinners and to give medicine for their infirmities, that same [charity] makes Him depart from His house when they have need, to visit and console them, so that they, receiving Him, might enjoy the *copious redemption*[247] that He won for them, and He receives contentment, seeing that His death and Passion do not depart in vain towards those whom He wants to visit.

But tomorrow we are not going with the Lord to visit the sick, but rather [we are going] to pleasures and feasts with Him. Certainly a very new thing for You, Lord, to go to walk about the streets, and with jubilations, and how much newer, inasmuch as it makes us admire and supplicate You, with great desire, to tell us the wherefore of such a new thing. But Your mercy does not permit this, our desire, to be born from that curiosity which is born in men from the natural appetite they have for knowing what fulfills them and what does not fulfill them. Neither do You permit it to be born from infidelity, wanting to know in order to believe. No, Lord, no, by who You are, let what is written not include us: *If they do not believe, they will not understand.*[248] We firmly believe—by Your gift—that what Your Church has ordained is inspired by God and very conforming to Your contentment and to our profit. But let us desire to know Your intention in this feast, to be more correct in celebrating it and going out with You, as we ought to, on the holy procession that the holy Church, inspired by You, has ordained for tomorrow.

The Procession of Corpus Christi, Recompense for Those [Processions] that Christ Made During His Passion

To this profitable and just question the words of our theme respond, although said many years ago by the prophet Isaiah, and in our tongue, they say this: *Because the soul of the Lord spent labor, He will*

---

[247] Ps 130:7.

[248] Cf. Is 7:9.

see, and He will be satisfied.[249] Brief words and a profound sentence, which the apostle Saint Paul declares with many, many more words, which are like a gloss to this text. They say this: *The Lord Jesus humbled Himself, made obedient unto death, and death on a cross; for this, the Father exalted Him and gave Him the name above every other name, so that, at the name of Jesus, every knee would bend, those of the heavenly as well as those of the earthly and those who are below the earth, and every tongue would confess that the Lord Jesus is in the glory of the Father.*[250]

A most just reward, certainly, and a very clear reason why that surpassing and ineffable goodness of God, which makes Him go so far that He gives Himself as reward, and an eternal reward, in payment for a jar of cold water given for love of Him[251]—and which comes from a pure heart and one which is in the state of grace; it is not just that the goodness which rewards, with such a reward, a little work done by a little man, would fail to reward the such great services, the such excessive labors, of Jesus Christ Our Lord, whose obedience and love made Him come as far as suffering a death in which were joined together such grave torments, such qualified dishonors, so that nothing equal to it has been found since the beginning of the world, nor will be found until its end.

And if to this greatness of service is joined the immense greatness and value of the person who suffered it, who is a divine person, we will see that there is not only a just reason, but an overflowing one, for why the Father would extol a man so much, giving Him the *name above every name*, a dignity above every dignity, *so that He would have princeship over all things.*[252] Also, making Him Lord of all that is created, He commanded that, either by desire or by force, every creature *in heaven and on earth and under the earth would*

---

249 Is 53:11.
250 Phil 2:8–11.
251 Mk 9:41.
252 Col 1:18.

bend the knee[253] in recognition of the supreme lordship, and that the honorable and pious name of *Savior of the world* be given Him, with much more reason than when Pharaoh gave it to the chaste Joseph;[254] he who was the figure of this Lord, not only in his singular chastity, but also in his being sold by his brothers and tossed into jail without fault, and in the great honor that he later received.

And from this it comes about that the heavenly Father wills that the steps of the sacred Passion, which, with much dishonor, Jesus Christ Our Lord suffered, be honored and solemnized in the holy Christian Church, in the seven canonical hours as in the altar-stone and altars and priestly vestments, in the holy sacrifice of the Mass, representing all and signifying, very particularly, the death of the Lord and its circumstances. Since the Most High Lord willed that, in all these things, we might make our honor and service correspond to the dishonor and sorrow with which His most blessed Son suffered *the Passion*, He suffers no reason why, the lesser things being honored with the peak of honor, the greater things would remain without correspondence.

And so that we might draw closer to our proposed theme, it behooves you to remember that, in past times, the Ark of the Covenant of the Lord did not stay in one place alone, but was first carried from the desert to the promised land and placed in Shiloh—which was quite a long trip—later, it was carried off by war and captured by the Philistines, in whose land it wandered from city to city; and

---

253 Phil 2:10.

254 Gn 41:45. In this verse, Pharaoh gives Joseph a new name, "Zaphenath-paneah" (RSV) or "Psonthom-phanech" (LXX). Jewish tradition has usually interpreted this name as "understander of secrets," "revealer of secrets," or "explainer of secrets;" based on newer studies of the ancient Egyptian language, many modern scholars instead interpret it as "the god speaks; he lives," or "the sustenance of the land is the living one." (This last interpretation is fitting in context, due to Joseph's role in saving Egypt from famine.) In the Vulgate, though, this verse reads, "And he changed his name and called him, in the Egyptian language, 'Savior of the world.'"

from there, it was brought to Beth-shemesh,[255] and from there to Kiriath-jearim, and later to Mizpah, and later to Gilgal; and later it was carried off, another time, by war, and it was also in Nob, and later in the house of Abinadab, and from there, David and all Israel brought it to the house of the Levite Obed-edom, and later, David made it pass by his castle, where he received it with much honor.

"Oh, dear God, Lord! Why so many processions with that Ark of Yours, when, if it had sense, it would have rested and complained about so many long and laborious moves?" This was not without reason, but, so that you might know that, just as that ark of wood and gilt was a figure of the sacred humanity of Jesus Christ Our Lord in very many things, so, too, it figured, with its many processions from one place to another, the many and very painful [processions] which the Lord had to make. Oh Lord, how well You fulfilled the figure of the ark by being the *Ark of divinity*, how well You fulfilled it in Your walking on more processions than it, and with Your great suffering and dishonor, the other ark not feeling either the one nor the other!

Our Ark walked, on the day of Holy Thursday, from Bethany to the sacred Cenacle[256] of Jerusalem, leaving His most sacred Mother there, full of pains, as He went on; and He walked a road of two miles, with steps enough to wear out her most delicate body, especially with the load of compassion that His sacred Mother carried. After this procession, which He made with His disciples, there followed another, from said Cenacle to the garden of Gethsemane, where He was arrested, which is two thousand three hundred and thirty-eight steps, which, since He was tired from the first journey, and from the labor of washing the feet of His disciples, and from the

---

[255] Throughout the following passage, I have used the versions of the Biblical names found in the RSV, rather than St. John's Spanish transliteration of the Vulgate versions. St. John's account confuses the travels of the Ark with the travels of Samuel, David, and the Israelites: after the Ark reached Kiriath-jearim, it stayed in the house of Abinadab there until David had it brought to Obed-edom's house (see 1 Sm 7:1–2; 2 Sm 6).

[256] That is, the Upper Room where Jesus celebrated the Last Supper.

great sadness that His soul felt, He could not finish walking without great tiredness.

But, in place of rest, the Lord is arrested, and with very ill treatment, He is brought uphill to the house of Annas, which was on the height of Mount Sion, a distance of eight thousand and odd steps; from there, he walked another forty-eight steps to the house of Caiphas, in which He was mistreated a great part of the night; and at the end of it, He was arrested and tied to a column in a most narrow jail. And after having been on foot all night, He walked, in the morning, another procession of one thousand three hundred and fifty-four steps, which was from the house of Caiphas to the house of Pilate. From there, He was brought to the house of Herod, which is one hundred and twenty steps; and, afterwards, He walked back, being handed over from Herod to Pilate. The labor of all this was so great that, if it were not by means of a miracle, the Lord could not have stayed on foot.

But if we compare the labor of the aforesaid processions with the last one—which still remained for Him to walk—from the house of Pilate to Mount Calvary, to end up, there, pouring out His blood and losing His life on the Cross for us, it will appear that, although the steps were very costly to Him, in comparison with this, they could be counted as light. That, Lord, that was a sorrowful procession, as You who walked it very well know, [that procession] in which, on top of the tiredness of the night and the day and on top of the weakness caused by the evil treatment of Your most sacred body that You received in the house of Pilate, with cruel blows, with sharp spines, and as Isaiah said, made completely *as if leprous*[257] and so maltreated, that, even if they put You next to a soft bed and even if they moved You only a little ways, and with much courtesy and care, this would be a grave suffering for You; and they do not act thus, but, adding suffering to suffering, they place upon Your most sacred shoulders two heavy pieces of wood, one of fifteen feet in

257 Is 53:4.

length, and another of ten, so that, like the beam of a press, they might squeeze and mill You; and they command You to go with this weight, not five or six steps, but one thousand eight hundred and seventy-two, which is how many there are from the house of Pilate to Mount Calvary.

Who could think that such cruelty could be performed? So it seems that, either the Lord did not feel pain in what He suffered, and for this reason, He could bear it, or, if He felt it, His love and His suffering were such as have never been seen nor will be seen. And so that evil men do not take the occasion to think that He did not feel it or that He felt it little, it was ordained by divine Providence that—so that we might grasp something of how grave were His sufferings, of how great was the tiredness of His divine Person, how heavy the Cross and how extreme the weakness of His most sacred body, that, if it was not for a miracle, He could not even walk, but merely live—when He began to walk a distance of twenty-five steps, the weight of the Cross pressed on the Lord so much that it brought Him to the ground, so that it would thus be publicly clear to all, those present and those to come, and even to His own enemies, who brought Him to be crucified, that the sufferings of the Lord were not a trick, but very true, since they did such a thing to Him.

And because this was so evident even to His enemies, they ordered that, so that life would not leave the Lord until He came to Mount Calvary, where they wanted to put Him on the Cross, and had died on it, they agreed to not put it on His shoulders again, and to put it on some man of much strength, who could carry it. But it was so heavy and carrying it was such a dishonor that, among many thousands of people who were there, not even one man was found who wanted to carry it for a plea, for money, for the respect of others; and they took the means of constraining Simon the Cyrene by force so that, although he did not want to, he would carry it and follow the Lord, who, although they took the heavy wood from off His shoulders because He rested on the road, they did not stop assailing with evil words and with disrespectful deeds, and proclaiming Him, with a loud, herald's voice, to be an evildoer, and not any such one, but a very well-known one; and, at the racket and proclaiming, the people went out of the doors of their houses, and others out of their windows, to see Him brought along, dishonored and afflicted, having very little compassion for Him and almost all delighting in it, and the main ones who mistreated Him saying that He had very well deserved it, and that they would give Him even greater torments, until His life was gone.

Oh most merciful Father! Oh, immense in goodness to reward even the small services that are done for You! Could Your heart suffer You to let so many and such long and costly processions pass without reward, especially that last one, which Your most blessed Son walked for Your obedience and for our profit, with such suffering and dishonor that no tongue can tell of it nor human nor angelic understanding grasp it? *This is not Yours*, Lord, since You are just and *You judge all the earth* in equality, as Abraham says.[258] And since His holy birth is celebrated with much honor, and the other acts of His life in diverse feasts, and also the particularities of His Passion in the holy sacrifice of the Mass, see, Lord, how, in payment for those processions—especially that which He walked to Mount Calvary—a most solemn procession is performed in all of Christendom on a day like tomorrow, in which [processions] Your most blessed Son goes out honored and surrounded by His vassals, as, there He went [surrounded] by His enemies, and how, in place of the lying proclamations that they then made of Him, tomorrow, devoted praises will be sung, which befit Him with much truth and justice.

Isaiah said, speaking of this Lord: *If He lays down His life for the remission of our sins, He will see a long* spiritual *generation*, which will proceed from Him.[259] Fulfill that promise, Lord, and command

---

[258] Gn 18:25.

[259] Is 53:10.

that we, those for whose sins He laid down His life, would go forth tomorrow in a procession with Him, confessing that the spiritual generation we have through Him is yielded to us, and that we, with a devoted offering of ourselves, would say to Him: "*Turn*, Lord, *Your eyes back and see that all of this people*, which goes here in procession, *has joined together and come to You* as to their true Lord and Redeemer.[260] *See*, Lord, and rejoice, and *let Your heart expand*[261] with the joy of having so many vassals who go out here with You, more determined to die for Your faith and for Your commandments than those of the other procession had hatred for You."

Let the priests go forth tomorrow—they whom He so honored that He chose them for His ministers—and let them carry Him on their shoulders with great reverence and love, holding themselves very favored in this, in recompense for the Savior carrying the Cross on His back, and all our sins upon Himself. Let the devoted Christians draw near to Him, honoring Him with such heart that they would cast their clothes on the ground before Him, so that the feet of those who carry the Lord might trample them, as they did who went with Him on the day of Palms. Let them see Him with much love and adore Him with great reverence, they who are in the streets and within their doors and windows. Let the priests go forth incensing Him; let the lay brothers dance before Him with devoted joy, as David did before the ark, and let the earth resound with great solemnity; and, with all care, let tomorrow's festivity be ordered so that, as a manifestation of divine Justice, which honors those obedient to it, none of the dishonors that were done to the Lord in the other procession might remain in this one, unless there corresponds to it an honor equal to or greater than the other dishonor.

This, then, Christians, is tomorrow's procession, singular and not celebrated on any other day; this is the cause and justification for it; this the sentiment with which it is to be celebrated, with memory

260 Is 60:4.

261 Is 60:5.

of and correspondence to—in a contrary way—the other, very bitter, procession which the Lord walked, in which, as the theme says, *He labored His soul* with grave anguishes, and His body with unspeakable sufferings, through which God the Father willed to see tomorrow, in the procession, such a crowd of faithful vassals, who proclaim, with devoted praises and services, that they are His, so that they might give the Lord satiety, rest, and consolation.

How to Celebrate the Sufferings of the Lord with Joy?

Now that this doubt is satisfied, another remains for us, no less worthy of asking nor less profitable to know, and it is this: With what heart and with what justification can we celebrate the memory of such sufferings with such joy? And this put Saint Anselm in a bind when he thought of it, and marveling, he said: "How, Lord, will I rejoice in having received salvation, since it was given me by Your sufferings? How will I enjoy my life, which cost You Your death?" This saint says this.[262]

And, certainly, it seems a strange thing for us to go out in procession tomorrow, singing and dancing, in memory of when the

---

262 St. John is referencing *Prayer* XLI of St. Anselm (or Pseudo-Anselm), though that saint's rhetorical questions are focused more on the insufficiency of his praise than on a feeling of guilt for his joy. So Anselm says, "Therefore, how will I praise You? In what way will I exalt You? With what emotion will I pray to You? With what jubilation will I glory in You? Through You, hell is despoiled, and it is cut off from all those redeemed by You. Through you, the demons are terrified, crushed, chained, and trampled. Through You, the world is renewed . . . Therefore, with what emotion will I glory in You, without Whom I would not only lack glory, but, furthermore, I would eternally have infernal sorrow and misery? With what delight will I rejoice in You, through Whom, in place of servitude in Tartarus, I am given the inheritance of the kingdom of the heavens? With what joy will I exult in You, without Whom I would be horrified even at this very moment, and through Whom I expect to well rejoice in eternity?" (PL 158:936A, 937A).

Lord went in another procession, carrying a heavy Cross on His back, tired and sweating, and even pouring out His precious blood on the road. Scripture says that *music in the time of weeping is an importunate thing* and heavy without reason.[263] And it doesn't seem like consolation to the afflicted one to leap and dance in memory of his labors; rather, if one looks closely, it seems more like an act of hatred than a work of love, since he who wills ill for another exults in seeing [his labors] and remembering them; but he who loves holds the labors of his friend as his own, and as such, he feels them and weeps over them, and even, many times, with greater feeling than that very friend who suffers them.

What is this, Christians? What is this that we have prepared for tomorrow: instruments, music, dancing and dances, an entire feast of much joy, without any mixture of sadness, when what is represented, in memory of which it is done, is a most great and purest pain, without any mark of joy? If they command us to represent that joyful procession that the holy Fathers made out of Limbo on the day of the Resurrection of the Lord, alongside His most blessed soul, unto the sepulcher, so that, from there, the Lord, resurrected and glorious in body and in soul, accompanied by men and angels, all full of joy, might go to visit and console His most sacred Mother, as He did, one would come very early in the morning to make many joyful gestures in our procession in memory of the other, greater [gestures] that were made in the other [procession]. But that those who have love for the very Lord who suffered would celebrate the memory of the sorrowful Passion with jubilation, that struck Saint Anselm, and it strikes everyone who has a desire to inquire into what is the cause of a correspondence full of such strangeness and inequality.

But, although it appears so to the human spirit, which does not know how to judge the things of God, the Church, taught by the Holy Spirit, commands us to celebrate this feast tomorrow

263 Sir 22:6.

in the way and with the joys with which we celebrate it, just as it appears in the *Clementina "Si dominum,"* whose holy words are these: "So the clergy with the people shall run together joyously to this festivity and exercise themselves in praises and songs of the Lord; and hearts, desires, mouths, and lips, all shall say songs of healthy joy. Faith shall sing, hope shall give leaps of joy, holy love shall exult, devotion shall give jubilant applause; and all the faithful shall join together with joyful heart and prompt will and shall set to work on their laudable exercises, celebrating the solemnity of such a great feast."[264]

Have you heard these words well? Since, with this joy so fulfilled, as I've told you, we are commanded by the holy Church to, tomorrow, carry the Lord through those streets, in memory of His sacred Passion, how will we be certain of doing this so that it be well done? Declare to us, Lord, this enigma, as Sampson declared his to his wife.[265]

And this ought to be the declaration of this doubt, that, in the Passion of the Lord, there are two things to consider: One is looking at it *in itself*; and according to this, it was very sorrowful and painful to the Lord who suffered it, and consequently, it ought to be so to all those who love Him well, and they ought to feel it with bitterness from the depths of their hearts, and even with tears from their eyes on the outside. And, to fulfill this so just obligation, and to celebrate

---

264 The reference is to the *Clementine Constitutions,* sometimes known as the *Liber Septimus [Seventh Book],* a collection of canon law promulgated by Pope Clement V (r. 1305–1314). *"Si dominum" [If the Lord]* are the first words of Book III, Title XVI, Chapter 1, which contains the bull *Transiturus de hoc mundo [When He was to pass out of this world],* which instituted the feast of Corpus Christi. The bull was promulgated on August 11, 1264, by Pope Urban IV (r. 1261–1264). For the full text of the bull, see *Clementinae: Clementis Quintae Constitutiones, quas Clementinas vocant…,* ed. Johannes de Imola (Lyons: Hugo a Porta, 1550), 132–137; the passage quoted by St. John is on page 135.

265 See Jgs 14:17.

this sorrowful memory with sorrow, the Church indicated the time of Holy Week, in which crosses are dressed in mourning and the altars change their ornaments, the Passion of the Lord is chanted four times, according to the four Evangelists who wrote it, and a sermon is made about it, and everything provokes one to a feeling of compassion and sadness, so that we might thus pay the service of devotion to the Lord who suffered for us. And we fulfill this first consideration by looking at the sacred Passion *in itself*, which was a cause of pains to the Lord and of compassion to us.

But if we look at it according to another consideration, in regards to *the effects* that proceed from it, in this way, we will find enough material to rejoice, just as, in the other, we found enough to sadden ourselves. A pitiful thing it is to think that Jesus Christ Our Lord, without owing anything, would die, and by death on a cross;[266] but if it is considered in this way, by the merits of this most precious death, millions of souls have resurrected since the beginning of the world, and will be resurrected until the end of it, from the death of sin to the life of grace; and after the general judgment, our glorious souls and bodies, joined together, will live forever, enjoying God in heaven, we will find much to delight in, and we will call it a happy death which caused so many and such precious lives. Because, if Saint Gregory calls original sin—because it is remedied by such redemption and by such a Redeemer—*happy fault*,[267] how much more will the very redemption and death of Christ merit such a name, [that death] which was not a fault, like that of Adam, but a punishment taken on without His own fault, with most fervent charity, in order to destroy the sins of others? *Abraham saw this day* in spirit, and *he delighted to see it*; [268] certainly not in the pains which the Lord had to suffer, but because he saw that, because of them, he

---

266 See Jgs 14:17.

267 A reference to the famous line from the Exultet at the Paschal Vigil: "O happy fault, which merited the having of such and so great a Redeemer!"

268 Jn 8:56.

was to depart from the death of sin to a life of grace and of glory, the worth of which there is no one who could feel or tell.

From the Passion Was Born Honor for Christ and Much Good for Us

And what more confirms the aforesaid is that, although the Lord knows how much our remedy was to cost Him, He not only did not flee it, but setting His eyes on remedying us and taking no account of the sufferings and death that it was to cost Him, He said, living in this life, with most fervent love of us: *With a baptism I have to be baptized. How afflicted He walked so that it would be effected!*[269] And so, when the day of His Passion came and He was bathed with His blood on the Cross, although Jeremiah said in His persona, *there is no suffering equal to Mine,*[270] yet, amidst those very sufferings, His love was so vivid for us, without repenting of it, without turning back from buying His servants at the price of His most precious blood and divine life, that, as Scriptures says, *the many waters* of sufferings *and* the abundant *rivers* of His precious blood *could not quench love,*[271] but He forever remained conqueror, and thus the Lord said: "If all this that I suffer for men is not enough for their remedy, I will suffer more and more." And since the delight that we take in someone's good is in proportion to the love we have for him, who could recount how much the Lord delighted in our good, although won at His great cost, since the love of Christ, as Saint Paul says, is greater than what can be known?[272]

So, Lord, Your *desire*, which *put You in such straits*, was fulfilled, and *Your day* came,[273] painful on the one hand, yet very delightful

---

[269] See Lk 12:50.
[270] Lam 1:12.
[271] Sg 8:7.
[272] See Eph 3:19.
[273] Is 35:5–6.

on the other, [the day] on which You did the greatest deed which was ever done, since You performed the greatest work of love, and with more love than the world has seen or will see, dying for Your slaves, not good [slaves], but traitors. And it is no marvel that, from such a most precious tree, most powerful and sweetest fruits would go forth, and those who were first captives would be rescued; those who were in darkness and blindness would gain the spiritual sight of faith; those who were weak and lame before would receive the swiftness of hinds to run the road of God with strength and with joy;[274] those who were imprisoned in jails of sins, *bound by iron and poverty*,[275] were freed; and as Saint Augustine says, *the only One died so to not stay one*;[276] he means to say, so He would have companions and brothers who would, jointly with Him, enjoy the name of sons of God and the hope of being heirs of heaven.

Who, considering these things, will not see how great a reason there is for goods of such value, precious and eternal, to be celebrated with the greatest delight within and without, as much for the honor of Jesus Christ Our Lord, who gained it for us, as for the most great good which came to us? This is the divine providence of the Most High Father, who has shown, with such effects and with such feasts, that they were liars, those who had evil feelings towards His only-begotten Son, when, bringing Him to be crucified and after crucifying Him, they said, "See the state of this man, His words, miracles, and the people who believed in Him: He, condemned to death; His disciples, fled, and everything, ended and lost."

May the lips that speak lies, Lord, *be confounded*[277] and their hearts blind, for they thought that His doctrine and His life was a human invention, and not Your work; let them know that, although they

---

274 Is 35:5–6.

275 Ps 107:10.

276 See St. Augustine, *Sermon* 171.5: *Mortuus est pro nobis Unicus, ne remaneret unus* (PL 38:935).

277 See Ps 31:18.

put Your only-begotten Son on a Cross and between two thieves, attempting to get Him wrapped up with those evildoers so that His memory would be forgotten like theirs, and so that there would be no man who would believe in Him, nor even dare to name Him, what was to be was completely the opposite to what they had thought, said, and attempted; and that all that they did not only failed to let them succeed in their evil intent, but that it was, as they say, like throwing grease on a fire, because Your most blessed Son was, and is, and will ever be, more honored and loved inasmuch as they did and desired to do more ill to Him, persecuting Him with rabid hate, and He suffering it with obedience to and love of You.

Let those evil men know, Lord, that, when they thought that the affairs of Your only-begotten Son were lost, at that time, they begin to re-green with divine force, which shines and manifests itself inasmuch more as there is less human favor and more human disfavor. Let this fire, lit by You, Lord, not be under the candlestick;[278] let it be published in the world; let all know the most precious and most abundant fruit that followed from Our Lord Jesus Christ dying for the good of men; let it go forth to the public, and let the people boast that He won, not by spilling another's blood with the lance of His hand, but by His own most sacred hands being broken with nails, and that He, with a new and never-before-seen manner of victory, by spilling His own blood and dying, was the conqueror.

Make it so, Lord, that, in place of a people who blasphemed Him and held His faith and those who believed in Him as ended, tomorrow let innumerable people go out in all the world, full of great jubilation, firmly believing in heart and devotedly confessing with mouth that, by the merits of the death and Passion of Jesus Christ Our Lord, they have received the sacred fire of Your faith, and knowing the Father, Son, and Holy Spirit as the one only and true God, and all the rest that the holy Catholic Church teaches.

---

278 Cf. Mt 5:15.

Tomorrow, too, let those many captives who were in diverse mortal sins go out with the Redeemer, giving thanks and confessing that, through the sacred Passion of Him, they were given succor, with which they did penance for their evil lives, by which the demon had held them captive, and through the mediation of the holy Sacraments that are in the Church, they received pardon and grace. Let those go forth, tomorrow, with the heavenly Doctor, and exulting with Him, those who have been healed, by the merits of His Passion, from long and spiritual infirmities, giving Him glory and thanks. And let everyone remember tomorrow, each one in particular, the time that the Lord suffered him to live in sin and in the dangers of body and soul from which He has freed him; the spiritual weaknesses and infirmities of which He has healed him; the good works that He has done to him; and giving thanks for all of this sacred Passion, the fount of all our good and remedy, let each one sing to the Lord, with devotion, that song of David: *My soul, bless the Lord, and all things that are within me, bless His holy Name; because He has been meek and pardoning of all your evils; and He heals all your infirmities, preserves your life, that it might not fall into death, and crowns you with mercy and mercies.*[279]

Let all of us go out, tomorrow, with this Lord, proclaiming that He is our true Creator and Shepherd, and *we*, by His grace, *are sheep of His flock,*[280] for He snatched us away from the mouth of the infernal wolf and won and saved us by His precious blood, and let us give Him thanks because He has freed us from the kingdom of sin, which held us subject, from the cruelty of the demon, from the pains of hell, and incorporating us into His Body, He has taken us as His brothers and has given us the hope of reigning in heaven with Him.

Who will not give leaps of joy, seeing that he has escaped the filthiness of the flesh, the bitterness of ill-will, the puffing of pride and of the other sins, in which he remembers how he used to walk,

[279] Ps 103:1–4.

[280] Ps 95:7.

and [seeing] that he has passed on to the purity of chastity, to the light of humility, and to the softness of charity, with which he loves the good in God and the evil for love of God? Who will there be who, considering that God has led him to suppose that He has pardoned him of his past sins, and as David says, *has estranged them from us as far as the East is from the West,*[281] will not sing with joy, "*Let those who are redeemed by the Lord from the hand of the enemy, and whom He has joined, turning them to Himself* from the sundry scatterings they were in before, *praise the Lord for His mercies and His marvels among the sons of men?*"[282] For thus act those who have been imprisoned many years, with feet chained and shackled, who, when they depart from there, do not grow tired of giving leaps of joy, of giving thanks to God, of exercising the limbs that were hindered before.

Then *let your voices be new, and your hearts and works,*[283] and renewing ourselves with the grace of the Lord and separating sin from us, however heavy it be upon us, let us run with Our Lord tomorrow, humble, devoted, and thankful, and so jubilant within and without that we would give the whole world to understand that we are so delighted and rich with having Him as Lord, and with the mercies that He has done to us, and with the hope of those He will do, that, so full of joy, we cannot contain ourselves either in our houses or in the temples; and so we go out across the streets and plazas to pour out, with exterior signs, the greatness of the delight that we feel within ourselves, accompanying, and giving glory to, and celebrating the triumph of the Lord who rescued us as captives, in a much greater way than those whom David rescued from the Amalekites, who went before him, and those who saw them said:

---

[281] Ps 103:12.

[282] Ps 107:2–3, 8.

[283] This is a quote from St. Thomas Aquinas's hymn *Sacris solemniis,* one of the many he wrote for the feast of Corpus Christi; in Latin, the lines read *Nova sint omnia, / corda, voces et opera.* The last stanza of *Sacris solemniis* is often sung as a separate hymn: *Panis angelicus.*

This is the spoils that David won.[284] Let all men, all the earth, see us tomorrow; let the angels and saints of heaven see us, and let them know that we are spoils, that Jesus Christ Our Lord rescued and won us, and let us carry Him in procession, giving thanks and confessing that He is our Creator and Redeemer, and let us hope that He will be our Glorifier.

And because we are not sufficient to do this as it ought to be done, let us beg earth and heaven to aid us in giving Christ the honor and thanksgiving that are owed Him.

How Great Ought to Be the External Signs of Our Joy Tomorrow

From the aforesaid, the response to the aforesaid question is clearly drawn forth, and it is this, that as, in Holy Week, we feel and weep for the Passion of the Lord, recounting how He was very pained for us and our sins, so, tomorrow, considering that the Passion of the Lord birthed honor and lordship for Him and great goods for us, we delight in Him and manifest, with external signs of joy, thanksgiving for the goods that came to us through His sacred Passion.

And, also, we will draw from this the measure with which we will take this delight tomorrow. Because, just as cause and effect are companions, so it is reasonable that neither the pain that is received through the sacred Passion be without some consolation, nor the delight that is received through its effects be alone, but that it go mixed up with the tender and sweet tears that are wont to be born from the memory of the Passion of the Lord. Those who delight in the Lord in heaven have a most just cause for drinking the wine of their joy pure, although they remember that they gained it by means of the bitterness of the Passion that the Son of God suffered for them; because they are sure that they will certainly never lose their joy, and they are certain that God does not want them to mix

284 1 Sm 30:20.

sadness with it, be it little or much; and even if they want to mix it, He does not agree with them, and for this reason, such an effect will not follow. Because just as, by the punishment of His justice, any joy, however small it be, will be forever far from those in hell; so, through His great mercy, sorrow, weeping, sadness, and anything that gives them pain, be it little or great, will flee very far from those who are in heaven.

This, brothers, is the language of heaven; but we who live in this exile, and do not know how long our perseverance will endure in the good, and since God has not forbidden—rather, He has commanded—us to take up salutary sadness, we ought to celebrate these holy festivities with delight in the good that we have; while also mixing our delight with fear, because we can lose it, and with sadness, although not unpleasant, through the sufferings that our delight cost the Lord.

This is no invention of mine, but rather a doctrine that the holy Church gives us in the aforesaid *Clementina*, teaching us, with the light of heaven, how we ought to celebrate tomorrow's festivity, through these words: "This is the glorious memory that swells the hearts of the faithful with salutary delight, and, jointly, gives them a devotion of tears. With joy, let us delight, and, with reason, let us make memory of that by which we were liberated; and, remembering the Passion of the Lord, through which this liberty came to us, we can restrain our tears [only] with difficulty, so that they do not run from our eyes. In such a way that, in this most sacred commemoration, we jointly have the delight of sweetness and the accompaniment of tears, because we delight while pouring forth tears and [we are] weeping while having joy, because the heart full of great delight distills sweet drops of water through its eyes."[285] The aforesaid *Clementina* says all of this, and out of this, we will take

[285] See the *Clementine Constitutions* III.XVI.1, in *Clementinae: Clementis Quintae Constitutiones, quas Clementinas vocant . . .*, ed. Johannes de Imola (Lyons: Hugo a Porta, 1550), 133–134.

the doctrine of temperance that our hearts will carry tomorrow; this is befitting, to wit, that they would go out delighting and tender, accompanying the Lord.

And it is also given us to understand that tomorrow is not a day of sorrowful representations of the Passion of the Lord, since it is not celebrated with the bitterness of Holy Week, but rather because of the good that [the Passion] caused, as we have said. And since such representations, being so holy in themselves, do not go well together with tomorrow's procession, by seeming untimely, it is clear that we ought even less to consent to other games that are indecent in every time; rather, everything should be in conformity with the contentment of that Lord, for whom the feast is celebrated. Because of which it is befitting, and very much so, that nothing, small or great, should be represented, done, or said, that is not examined by a grave and wise person, and one who is not merely content with there not being a word of error in these things; rather, he should also manifest no dishonesty, and he should have a Christian feeling and the spirit of the Lord, in order to taste what songs and representations will please this Lord, for whom the feast is celebrated; since He is very grave and honest, and every idle word, every deed that is not accompanied by much honesty, seems evil to Him, it is clear that what does not seem good to Him in any time or place will seem worse in His holy day, procession, and presence.

I have seen and heard grave errors surrounding this, and it ought to be examined closely whether the person to whom this examination is permitted is highly qualified, and it is found to be commanded, by grave persons, that nothing is to be done or said on this nor on other festivities without being examined by him, because, done otherwise, it would renew the pains of the Lord's Passion rather than give Him delight in seeing its effects worked in us.

And let this be notorious to all, to claim that what the Lord intends in all His works and festivities is only that we should receive vain joy, from which some injury to the soul ordinarily follows, rather than the profit of our souls and our sanctification; and, because of this, everything ordered in feasts will have to conform to this end.

Lord, Where Are You Going?—I Am Seeking My Brothers

This profit of our souls brought Him from heaven to earth; it placed the Cross on His shoulders; and, to him who asks Him, going down the street of bitterness, laden with [the Cross], "Lord, where are you going? And why are You going along, treated so differently than You deserve?" The Lord will answer him what Joseph answered when his father sent him to visit his brothers, and walking outside the path, someone asked him who he was looking for, and he answered, *I am seeking my brothers.*[286] Oh, dear God, and how far outside the path did the Lord walk that day, since suffering punishment does not befit him who has no fault, and dying is not something that befits the immortal! But, His justice and His omnipotence looking out, the Lord took up these works, so strange to Him, and He embraced them in order to work His mercy for men, *for it is His work,*[287] very much His own, as Isaiah had prophesied it, that in order for the Lord to work His own work, *He worked things strange to Himself;*[288] and that going out of His own path, and what appears to be going outside of the path was, instead, entering more into it, since the

[286] Gn 37:16.

[287] Is 62:11.

[288] The Vulgate of Isaiah 62:11 begins: *ecce Dominus auditum fecit in extremis terrae [behold, the Lord made it known in the farthest reaches of the earth].* St. John seems to be skipping the word *auditum* ("heard"), to make the phrase read, "The Lord acted in the farthest reaches of the earth." He then interprets "farthest reaches" (*extremis*) to mean "outside of what is his own" or "strange." Thus, he reaches the paraphrase, "He worked things strange to Himself," and thus he has the idea of the Lord acting "outside of His own path," that is, outside of what is typical and befitting for Him.

works of His mercy are more honorable to Him and more profitable to men, and because of this, we make use of them.

Men were outside of their own path—which is the law of God—and, as Isaiah says, *All of us are erring, each one on his own side, like lost sheep*;[289] and if the pious Lord did not depart from the path of His rest and immortality (not so that He would lose what He had, but so that He would take on the sacred humanity, mortal and passible,[290] in order, by means of it, to pay for the faults of the erring and those off the path), He would never meet them, nor would He draw them to the path, nor would He win them in this way.

I've said all of this so that you might know that that same desire of seeking us and sanctifying us which drew Him out of the most secret bosom of the Father, where He was invisible and impassible, and that made Him human, subject to labors and death in this world, and made Him preach in temples, in houses, in streets, in plazas and mountains, on earth and at sea, inviting men with the remedy that He brought for all the evils they had, and pleading them to prepare themselves, through penitence, to enjoy the sweetest fruits of His life, labors, and death, which are eternal salvation—that same desire will, tomorrow, draw Him from His house, which is the temple, and from His tabernacle, where He is hidden, to go through our streets in procession.

And to him who marvels at this and asks Him, "What draws You, Lord, to walk about our streets of earth, vile and narrow, since You have as Your own the vastness of heaven in which to do it? Isn't it enough that You walked about the promised land with much tiredness, living in mortal flesh, without—now that You have an immortal and glorious body, and one which is seated in heaven

---

289 Is 53:6.

290 Philosophically and theologically, *passible* means "able to suffer" or "able to be acted upon." Traditional theology, based on Greek philosophy, says that divinity is *impassible* while created things are *passible;* in order to be able to suffer for us, God the Son had to take on *passible* humanity.

at the right hand of the Father—wandering through the streets of our exile, which are not Your own path, since, by being a place of corruption, they are not a place for a glorious body, one which is incorruptible?" Do you know what the Lord will respond to him who asks Him this? "I know all this; but I want you to know that, just as the Father sent Me, through My Incarnation, to visit men, and I wandered paths strange to Me in order to remedy them, so by My Father's command, I will depart from My tabernacle and go through these streets *to seek My brothers*, to give them the fruit of My death, which I suffered with most fervent love for them."

Oh, sweetest bowels[291] of ineffable love! Oh loving fire, for you always burn and never go out! Oh Heart wider than heaven, to suffer us and to place us in itself and to seek what fulfills us! Who will recount the paths that You take to seek the remedy, even for those who flee from You? You are so full of desire for our good, so great is the love that reigns in Your heart, that it seems like You won't fit in Your temple tomorrow, however big it be, and that the people who will go there to see You at Mass will seem few to You, with the desire You have of embracing all; and it is a shame that those who do not go to You are lost, and like an anxious mother and one covetous for a remedy for her children, You go out to the streets and public places and, as it is written, You preach in public and cry out in the plazas, saying, *If anyone is very little, let him come to Me.*[292]

Oh eternal Wisdom of the Father, how quietly it seems You go, set on a bier, under the curtains and accidents of bread! But he who is worthy of receiving from You spiritual eyes and sight, so that he could penetrate as far seeing Your most loving heart, and who has such spiritual ears so that they could hear You—such a one

291 While, in English, we often speak of the heart as holding the depths of our feelings, many languages instead speak of the bowels or guts. (Thus we do, in English, have the term "gut feeling"). In Biblical and Patristic Greek, for instance, a common term for compassion is literally "good bowels" (εὐσπλαγχνία).

292 Prv 9:4.

would understand that, just as when You lived in this mortal life, You preached and declared with a loud voice, *If anyone is thirsty, let him come to Me and drink*,[293] and *Come to Me, all you who labor and are burdened, for I will give you rest*,[294] that same thing that Your tongue said then, Your heart says now, while going about on the bier. Because, although Your voice was heard then, and is not now, yet Your love, with which You spoke then and with which You now go forth in such a way, is one, which [love] does not let You rest and moves You to seek one means after another until You finish Your desired work of the good of men. Because, although You have finished with Your Eternal Father, who pardons and receives into His grace sinners who convert to Him through penitence, and achieving this cost You Your life, yet, if man does not prepare himself to receive this grace, nothing that You gained on the Cross will profit him. And, because of this, Lord, this task still remains for You now, to finish with men, so that they will want to receive pardon and grace, which they have to beg for, walking after You and even laboring until death, so that You would give it to them.

You find, Lord, this hardness of heart that is in men, because of which they do not want to receive, begging, that for which they have to beg and give their lives; this takes You from Your own home and brings You through their streets, giving loudest cries from Your heart: "*Come to Me, all* you who are lost: enjoy My redemption, for I will give you remedy for whatever ill you have!"

And just as, back then, Lord, when You went out through the streets, You healed the sick, converted sinners, and did other works of mercy to those who wanted to receive them, so too, if now, there is someone who hears Your going out on those walks tomorrow with that same love with which You walked about when You lived a mortal life, and when You went, with the Cross on Your back, to suffer for men, and if they hear Your going about, saying from Your

---

293 Jn 7:37.

294 Mt 11:28.

heart, "Here I am, men, in this procession, as a testimony that I do not regret having walked the other [procession] to Mount Calvary, sweating and spilling blood for your remedy, and, if it is necessary to, once again, suffer what I suffered there and to die on the Cross once again, I will do and suffer all that is asked of Me so that your soul will not be lost, but rather might attain eternal salvation," who, Lord, hearing this, could defend himself against Your stubborn request of love? And, seeing that You go out to seek in the streets even those who do not go to seek You in Your temple, and You go to invite, by the sight of You, even those who do not want to see You, who could remain without handing his whole heart over to the obedience of Your commandments and casting away all sin from himself? Woe to such hardness that impedes such great goods, and that makes the Lord go forth in vain to pass through our streets, which He did to fulfill His accustomed office of healing the sick and sinners who come to Him!

Remember how the holy Gospel recounts that [when] the Lord [went] to resurrect a dead girl, *accompanied by many people*, there came up from behind Him a woman, sick *for a time of twelve years, who had spent her estate in curing herself*, and what she had received from the cure was that, first being rich and sick, she became sick and poor and without hope of human remedy; but she found it in Jesus Christ Our Lord, *saying in her heart, "If I could* come *and touch the fringe of the garment of this Lord*, I trust in Him that *I would then gain salvation*;" she came and touched and, in touching, was healed, the mercy of Christ corresponding to the heart of the good woman; He asked those who were there, *"Who touched Me?"* And Saint Peter responded: Master, the multitude of people presses in on You, and do You say: "Who touched Me?" To which the Lord responded, letting it be understood that He did not call pressing in on Him "touching Him:" *Someone touched Me, for I have felt power depart from Me.*[295]

---

[295] Mk 5:21–34; Lk 8:41–48.

Oh, so great the mercy this Lord does to us in the procession tomorrow, for there were some hearts, desirous of salvation, devoted to the Lord, trusting in His mercy, who were cured by Him! That many who are sick in their souls will go out tomorrow with Him, there's no need to doubt. Some will bring infirmities of mortal sins (may the mercy of God deliver us from them!); others, venial; others, evil inclinations and evil customs, which perhaps have persisted for twelve years, just as infirmity of the body did in that woman, and it could even be for longer. And the omnipotent Doctor will come near us with a great will to cure us, and beseeching us with the cure, and even paying us so that we might want to cure ourselves; and, there being no one to *touch Him*, as that woman touched Him, the procession being finished and we taking stock of ourselves, we find that we bring home our sins and evil inclinations as whole as they were before; and God forbid that we return home worse than we were.

Do you know, brothers, what it is *to touch* the Lord in order to gain salvation from Him? To believe in Him with the Catholic faith, to know one's own sins, to be heavy-hearted for having done them, to propose amendment and confession, to have confidence that, through the wounds which Jesus Christ Our Lord suffered in His sacred body, hands, and feet—which is *the fringe of His garment*—one will receive pardon for his sins and salvation from His wounds, and that, going out to the procession as evil and sick, one will return justified and with salvation for his soul.

Oh Lord, what a happy procession and hour it is for You when You find, in those streets, *a lost sheep* who leaves his sins and flees to You, and consents in Your taking him upon Your shoulders and carrying him to Your Church, and confessing and communing, he is joined with the others of Your flock, who are in Your holy grace and love. Oh, how many such ones will be gained in tomorrow's procession!

We Press in on Him and We Do Not Touch Him

But, oh sorrow! For I fear greatly that it will happen as Saint Peter said, *that the companies press in on the Lord,*[296] and pressing in on Him, do not touch Him. Those people gladly went out accompanying the Lord, and so that each one might get closer to Him, some pressed in upon the others, and they pressed in upon the Lord; and, touching Him so much with their bodies, no one profitably touched Him except that woman. Have you looked on and wept as the same thing happens with us, to the letter? We go through the streets with the Lord with much jubilation and contentment; we snag the closest spot in order to go along next to Him; and, sometimes, you have seen or heard [it told] that, in the temples and in the processions, there are contentions, and even worse, over who will be in the most honored spot and the one closest to the Lord (this is a very irreverent thing, and it will be well punished!) and, in going out like this, the soul being careless in feeling the sweetness of the presence of the Lord who goes there, drunk upon seeing the exterior jubilations and games, disordered, unprepared, without pureness of soul, without sorrow for sins, without wanting to profit from that omnipotent power, [which is] powerful to remedy all ills, we offer to the Lord the whole body with which we make our presence and accompaniment there, and we go away from Him with our soul; and, in this way, although we go near, *we press in upon Him and do not touch Him.*

Do you want to see this more clearly? What is it to *press in upon a body*, except to want to make it fit into a smaller space than that which is just and due to it? And, just as the place where the immense God will dwell in us has to be [fit] for esteeming Him, reverencing Him, and loving Him without tax and beyond all measure, loving Him beyond all the things of earth and heaven, and loving Him more than ourselves, if you, Christian, do not

---

296 Lk 8:45.

give God your heart widened with the greatness and wideness of this reverence and love, then you want to put Him in a little place, you want to own Him with little love, and He will complain and say: *He who loves father or mother more than Me is not worthy of Me.*[297] And if you are an infidel who lacks love and faith, we would say: "God has no place there in which to repose; and, in the heart and understanding of a man like that, God is as if He were not;" because, without true faith, which is the foundation and principle of every good, there is no esteem nor love for the Lord. But you, who, on the one hand, have the Catholic and true faith, and celebrate this holy festivity tomorrow by accompanying and reverencing the Lord, and on the other hand, do not bear in your soul that spiritual wideness of heart, loving the Lord above all things, you come to Him with faith, you come to Him with the body, you come to Him with bodily ceremonies no more; you badly press in upon Him; and when He sees you, He will not be able to say, in truth, *he will see and he will be satisfied*;[298] but He still has the greatest hunger to see your soul placed in a state of grace and [to see you] returning home freed of the sins that you carried to the procession.

It is a great sorrow that, going with the Lord who wants you and can unburden you of the heavy load of your sins, which is enough to carry a man to hell, you yourself would rather remain in a state of condemnation, with your sins on your back, instead of being liberated and running, by means of the commandments of God, with the swiftness of a hart.

But what is even worse and more sorrowful, and what is enough to make a Christian heart that has love for the Lord burst with sorrow, is that, on the very feast of His most sacred Body, in the very presence of the Lord Himself, on that day ordained so that He *would see and be satisfied* and rest *in payment for what His soul labored*

297 Mt 10:37.

298 Is 53:11.

in His sacred Passion,[299] there, there you offend Him, Christian, and without any shame, you raise your eyes, which should have been fixed on Him, and you fatten them on the *faces* of women, and your heart in lusting after them. And if into this shamelessness fall not only the common folk—who, as Jeremiah says, *perhaps do not know the judgment of the Lord*[300]—but also the leading men (and how much more if he is an ecclesiastic!) who, the ones and the others, ought to have better understood and put into action the will of the Lord: who will have a heart to suffer this, who a tongue to speak of this, except to say with Jeremiah, *behold, these ones have further shattered the yoke and broken the chains of the commandments of the Lord. Who will give water for my head, and, for my eyes, founts of tears, and I will cry day and night for the dead of the daughter of my people? Who will bring me to solitude, where the walkers pass by, and I will forsake my people, and I will separate myself from them, because they are adulterers and joined to sinners?*[301]

Oh, the holy and solemn day of the Body of Jesus Christ Our Lord, and how little rest and satiety do you give Him on it, and how little gain of souls, by being ill-prepared for what we celebrate! Oh Christian army of the great Captain Jesus Christ, how forceful you were wont to be in conquering the passions of the flesh, in denying your own will, and how gladly you offered yourselves to death in honor of your Lord! Who, in a miserable, so flimsy exchange, made it so that, for one Lord's day, for one moment and in the presence of the Lord Himself, you don't have the strength to leave off looking at and lusting after a woman, while you have the humanized God before you, upon whom, with much reason, with great profit and delight, you could fatten your sight today and employ all the love of your heart? Why do you do just the opposite? Don't you know that you came out here today to bear witness

299 Is 53:11.
300 Jer 5:4.
301 Jer 5:5, 7.

that, through the Passion of Jesus Christ Our Lord, God the Father *has freed you from the power of darkness and led you to the Kingdom of the Son,*[302] which is purity, grace, and justice? And how will it be said of you that you are *the prey* and spoils *which* our *David freed* from the power of the Amalekites[303] if, by the sin in which you are in, the demon holds you in cruel captivity, and you are made his miserable prey, causing to be lost in you the many things which the Lord labored to gain for you, so that, seeing you, He would receive rest; and, in place of this, you press in upon Him with the hardness of your heart, you give Him grief, as much as you can, with new wounds?

And although He is, it seems to you, keeping quiet in the Sacrament, yet, in truth, He is complaining about the cruelty they commit against Him, as it is written: *him whom you wounded, they persecuted, and to the suffering of my wounds they added suffering.*[304] The Eternal Father wounded Him for our sins, and He gave Himself so that divine Justice would be content and satisfied by what the Lord suffered for them; and, this being the reason why, tomorrow, you should offer Him a heart confessed, communed, and adorned with good works, in which He might rest from His past labors, and see your purity and virtue, and *be satisfied*, you give Him, in place of this honey, bitterest gall, renewing His ancient wounds with the new [wounds] of new sins that you commit on His feast. And *wound upon wound*[305] is a thing of great suffering; and so it is [painful] for the Lord to find you ungrateful towards the benefice of His love and of the blood which He poured out for you. And, having sowed grapes of sweetest benefices in you, you make the fruit He gathers be thistles and thorns.

---

302 Col 1:13.
303 1 Sm 30:20.
304 Ps 69:26.
305 Jb 16:14.

Shame, shame, Christians, for such great ugliness! Compassion, compassion for how the soul of the Lord labored in His procession to Mount Calvary and death on the Cross! Let us labor, although it costs us our life, to cease from sins and go forth so humble, peaceful, and devoted, and such that the Lord, upon seeing us, would *see* and *be satisfied.* There is none, among however many of us go forth there, however small he be, for whom Christ did not die; let there be no one, big or small, man or woman, who does not go out there with thankfulness for this mercy and with a pure conscience.

Especially do the leading men, ecclesiastics and seculars, have this obligation, those who so much ought to exceed their inferiors and to be singular in serving and pleasing this Lord with better virtues, inasmuch as they are more singular in having received mercies from Him and in representing the person of God through the public office that they received from Him. And, since they are not particular persons, they are not content with their particular good; but, if they want their modesty and devotion, which they will carry [with them] tomorrow, to be of double merit and reward, let them not consent in other people's going forth as they ought not, lest they lose their own good through another's evil; since, of [men] such as these, it is said that "to not resist is to consent and approve."

Devotion, Charity, and Purity

The priests who will carry the great Lord tomorrow, Him whom the angels adore and revere, let them thank Him greatly, because He wants to be served by their shoulders, and by their suffering heat, by their sweating; and let them hope for a very great reward for this from the most liberal Lord whom they carry upon themselves, and let them remember the labor that the Lord expended, carrying them and everyone upon His shoulders on the day of His Passion, and let them take strength to suffer their own with much patience and even with joy; and let them beware lest it be more due to a fault of devotion than of bodily strength that they greatly feel the weight of the journey, the heat of the sun, the length of the path—which would be a very shameful thing.

The laymen who have estates, let them tomorrow give [money] for the rescue of some captive,[306] or let them take out of prison someone imprisoned because of debts, in honor of and thanksgiving for the blessed redemption from our spiritual captivity and the freedom from the chains in which our sins held us, so that they might celebrate in tomorrow's procession. To marry off an orphan girl[307] would also be fitting for this holy feast, since, on it, we celebrate the procession and day on which the Lord washed His Church with His blood and took her for His bride. And it would also be very *à propos* to give food to the poor and to refresh the sick, to clothe the naked, in honor of this sacred meal, which is so piously bestowed on us as a refreshment for our soul and body, for copious salvation from our infirmities, as clothing, house, and coat, and generally, as remedy for all our needs.

And, so that these works of mercy might be better done, the brothers[308] of this Most Holy Sacrament ought to burden themselves with them and, on tomorrow's feast, and during the whole octave, to ask for alms from the faithful in order to effect them; and the faithful [ought] to be very lavish in giving from their temporal

---

[306] See the reference to slavery among the Moors, above, along with its accompanying footnote (footnote 64).

[307] An orphan girl would not have a family to provide a dowry for her marriage, so St. John is encouraging the rich to pay for the dowries of such girls.

[308] This refers to the brothers in a Confraternity of the Most Holy Sacrament, not a religious order; such Confraternities are groups of the faithful, laymen and clerics alike, particularly devoted to the Blessed Sacrament. The first such Confraternity was founded by Franciscan fathers Cherubino di Spoleto and Bernardino Tomitano in 1484. See Benito, José Antonio, "La Cofradía del Santísimo Sacramento," Zenit, June, 17, 2012, https://es.zenit.org/2012/06/17/la-cofradia-del-santisimo-sacramento/ (accessed September 25, 2023).

goods, for the love of the Lord and to the same Lord, since He give His life for them.

And he who has no estate to serve the Lord with it, perhaps he will have suffered some evildoing from his neighbor, or he will have expended labor in suffering his evil condition. And if such a one pardons him who has angered him and suffers, with patience, the cross of another's evil condition, he should think that, tomorrow, he has offered the Lord, not an estate, but rather the blood of his own heart, since this hurts much more than that. Let the sick or poor man offer patience to the Lord tomorrow, and let him accompany Him, conforming himself to His holy will and giving Him thanks for everything.

The ones and the others should be able to carry such pure hearts (upon which God gazes) that the bodily eyes with which they gaze upon the Lord would give Him a pleasing sight with which He is content; since, just as *the pure of heart will see God*[309] in heaven with spiritual sight, so bodily sight which gives the Lord contentment on earth has to come from purity of heart. And, because this purity avails much, and few people know how to attain it by way of contrition alone and the intention of confession, the holy Church counsels us, as we have said in another sermon, that, since last Sunday, we should prepare ourselves with good works and pure confession of our sins, in order to receive Our Lord, to worthily celebrate His feast, and to enjoy the fruits of His Passion.

No Reward Will Be Lacking to Him Who Accompanies Him Well

And let it not seem a hard thing to you, neither the small nor the great, to do what has been asked of you in order to worthily celebrate this holy procession. Because if King David gave, as a reward, *bread,*

---

309 Mt 5:8.

meat, and buñuelos[310] to those who accompanied the procession of the Ark of the Old Testament, Jesus Christ Our Lord will give much better rewards to those who accompany His divine Person, signified by the passing of the other Ark. David was a temporal king, and he gave a little reward, and for things of little value; but the riches of our King are most precious and are eternal; and the wideness of His heart in giving exceeds any gain that a man will receive. Give to the Lord, brothers, what He asks of you, so that you would go out, as you ought, in His holy procession; and, in place of the *meat* and *bread* that David gave, He will give you His sacred body and His most precious blood, and His soul and divinity, all of which you receive when you commune; and happy is he who well receives it, because in this good are enclosed so many goods, without count, that, if a man labored all his life with good works, he would be very well paid by Our Lord's entering one single time into his chest.

And this Holy Sacrament, well-received, will not only give maintenance and strength to your soul, as *bread* and *meat* give to the body; but also, in place of the *buñuelos* that David gave, which are more *fruit* than maintenance, this Lord will give you, celebrating, as I've said, His procession, and receiving His holy body, a spiritual recreation, a feeling of your being unburdened of the weight of bad conscience, which will cause you greater delight than all the *fruits of the world.* And you can also count as *fruit* the holy indulgences and days of pardon that are conceded to those who celebrate these feasts, because, although the remission of the pains of Purgatory—which is granted for these and other indulgences—be a great thing, and very to be esteemed, yet, in comparison with the eternal glory which is promised for good works, that is *fruit*, and this is a *meal.*

And although any reward from among the aforesaid is enough to feed you and strengthen you to do all that is asked of you on behalf

---

310 2 Sm 6:19. *Buñuelos* is a type of fritter or doughnut common in Spanish-speaking countries; the Vulgate of this verse describes this food as "wheat flour fried in oil."

of Our Lord to go out tomorrow, as you ought, accompanying Him on His procession, yet, if, because of your lukewarmness, this is not enough, I beg you, for love of Our Lord, that you remember those processions which will be made eternally, not in the muddy and rocky streets of this exile, but in the wide plazas of the heavenly Jerusalem, so precious and pure that Saint John says that they are *pure gold*;[311] and there *the Lamb Who sits in the midst of the throne* will take His blessed sheep who will dwell there, and *He will lead and bring them to the fonts of the water of life*;[312] and, as the same Saint John says, *henceforth there will be no hunger nor thirst, nor will sun nor heat fall upon them;*[313] *and the Lord will wipe away their tears from their eyes; and there will be no more death, nor weeping, nor clamor, because all these things passed away*, without appearing there anymore.[314]

Does it not seem to you, brothers, that suffering the heat once a year, in order to accompany this holy procession, is well-spent in exchange for heat never more giving you pain, nor ever more having weeping, nor death, nor anything that looks like it? Does it not seem to you well-spent that the leading men and those who rule the people would go forth tomorrow, confessed and communed, and with reverence and a good example, as I've asked of them, honoring the Lord, so that, in those processions, the Lord might honor them and, as He has promised, *set them over all His goods*?[315] How well-paid there [in heaven] will be the work of mercy that you do tomorrow, in honor of this holy procession, pardoning him who has offended you, or giving food to the poor, clothing the naked, rescuing the captive, with other similar works, since, in payment for them, God will make you a participant in that grand, eternal, and ineffable mercy that He has promised to do there for those who work mercy

311 Rv 21:18.
312 Rv 7:17.
313 Rv 7:16.
314 Rv 21:4.
315 Mt 24:47.

here! Just as Jesus Christ Our Lord won this for us with His precious death and Passion, living in this mortal life, so He Himself, reigning in heaven and seated at the throne of glory which the Eternal Father gave Him, will put us in possession of the glory that He will have given us, and preserve us in it, since He is *Judge of the living and the dead,*[316] and majordomo of His Father, to whom it was given *to pay the daily wage to the laborers.*[317]

This Lord will go *before His sheep,*[318] because He has more glory than men and angels; and all of them will follow Him as sheep their shepherd, servants of the Lord and members of His head; and He will bring them in procession *to the fonts of the waters of life,*[319] which are the three divine Persons, who have one and the same and only essence; and there they will be satisfied, refreshed, and rested, seeing God face to face, loving Him and possessing Him without any end; where they will consider well-spent what they suffered for Him and did for Him here; and the same thing will we ourselves do if we prepare ourselves to be who we ought, and to carry Jesus Christ Our Lord on procession with us tomorrow, with due reverence, so that He would bring us, later, into the company of His procession in glory, *to which may He lead us.*[320] *Amen.*

---

316 Acts 10:42.

317 Mt 20:8.

318 Jn 10:4.

319 Rv 7:17.

320 *Ad quam nos perducat.*

Part 3

They Who Keep Vigil and Keep Us Awake

Sermon 63

Who Would See This Girl Fight with God!

(November 21: Presentation of Our Lady, Ws 8:22–35; Mt 1:1–16)[321]
Given in a Convent of Nuns

"Quid faciemus sorori nostrae in die quando alloquenda est?" "What will we do with our sister for the day when they are to speak to her?"[322]

Exordium

WE must come to the festivities of the most sacred Virgin with fervent and very thankful hearts. For this reason, Saint Bonaventure says that those who speak of Our

[321] In St. John's time, the Feast of the Presentation of Mary was still quite new, having been introduced to the Roman Missal in 1472. The Missal at that time stated, "On the Feast of the Presentation of the Virgin Mary, the Mass of the Nativity is to be said, changing the name 'Nativity' to the name 'Presentation.'" See *Missale Romanum noviter impressum . . .* (Venice: Lucas Antonius de Giunta, 1519), 260r. The feast was then suppressed by Pope Pius V in 1568, reintroduced by Pope Sixtus V in 1585, and then elevated by Pope Clement VIII in 1597. Clement's elevation of the feast (to the rank of "greater-double") also included a re-arranging of the feast, so that the Common of Mary, rather than the Nativity of Mary, became the base text of the feast. The readings in the Common are Sirach 24:14–16 and Luke 11:27–28.

[322] Sg 8:8.

Lady must have very great truth and fervor in their words:[323] *truth*, because the Virgin is the enemy of liars and a friend of those truthful in their words and works. This Lady is she who engendered a Truth who destroyed all heresies and a light which enlightened all darknesses. *Fervor*, because, if we do not love she who is truly ours, whom will we love? Saint Bernard says: "There is nothing that pleases me as much as speaking of this blessed Virgin, nor that frightens me as much as considering her greatness."[324]

This Lady who is now so great in the heavens was, for some time, a little girl here on earth; and, truly, she will be a little girl for those who are now true little children in her eyes, and who humble themselves and ask grace from her.

Why Does the Girl Enter the Monastery?

Our sister is a little girl. What will we do for the day when they are to speak to her in the person of patriarchs and of prophets and of all men?[325] Today these words are said: *Our sister is a little girl; how will we prepare her for the day when they are to speak to her?*

---

[323] See Conrad of Saxony, *Mirror of the Blessed Virgin Mary,* Prologue: "But, certainly, I think my insufficiency is in every way too great for this work, because of the excessive *incomprehensibility* of such *a matter*, because of the excessive *thinness* of my *knowledge*, because of the excessive *dryness* of my *tongue*, because of the excessive *unworthiness* of my *life*, and because of the excessive praise and *praiseworthiness of the person to be praised.*" See *Speculum Beatae Mariae Virginis Fr. Conradi a Saxonia* (Quaracchi: Typographia Collegii S. Bonaventurae, 1904), 1–2. This work was long attributed to St. Bonaventure before scholars determined that its author was actually Conrad of Saxony, a thirteenth-century Franciscan friar.

[324] See St. Bernard, *On the Assumption of the Blessed Virgin Mary, Sermon* 4.5: "Indeed, there is nothing that delights me more, nor which terrifies me more, than speaking of the glory of the Virgin" (PL 183:427D).

[325] *Soror nostra parvula est, et ubera non habet. Quid faciemus sorori nostrae in die quando alloquenda est?* Sg 8:8.

Today the holy mother Church celebrates that Lady who said in her canticle: *The Powerful One has done great things in me.*[326] We celebrate the feast of her presentation, the day on which her blessed parents, Saint Joachim and Saint Ann presented her—this Lady being a girl of three years—to the temple, so that she might serve the Most High God in the company of the maidens who served there. There was a house, incorporated into the temple in the manner of monasteries today; there the noble[327] maidens were placed to serve the Lord and be taught in knowledge and fear of Him. It was a holy seminary, and after they came of age, they took the state of married women. The reason why they presented her was because, when they were sterile, they promised that, if God would give them fruit, they would offer [the child] to Him, keeping her in full seclusion until she took the state of a married woman. Her parents presented her in the temple.

"Why do you, Lord, want her to enter at three years old, to be enclosed, to not walk through the streets?" Because those who are to receive God and to deal with Him should not be careless, but, rather, they should know that they have to prepare with much care in order to receive Him. In order for God to give the Law to Moses and to tell it to the people, God commands him that, three days before, they should not approach their women, and [He commands] many other preparations of sanctity;[328] how much more reasonable is it that he who is to receive God and deal with Him should prepare himself? Tell me now: if you were to toss a bit of balsam or other very excellent liquor into a vase, would you not first check if the vase is dirty or leaking, so that it would not be lost? So if you examine the vase before doing such a thing, how much more reason for [examining yourself] before receiving God?

---

326 Lk 1:49.

327 The word is *principal*; in *Sermon* 37, this word was used in the phrase *la gente principal*, "the leading people." Thus, the maidens discussed here would be those from the leading families of the town, or from the nobility.

328 See Ex 19:10–15.

"Why does the Girl enter the monastery?" Because a day will come on which she will receive God in her bowels. A day will come on which she will handle Him with her hands and be Mother to Him. God does not want His precious things to be in the sight of all. And if God wills that she who was secure in her house and in the streets and plazas to be enclosed, what will He do to us who are ready to fall?

"Why do You enclose her, Lord?" So that she might be an example to men and women; to make them understand that, if God willed that she who was secure would detach herself from what is not befitting, how necessary it is that we flee [such things]. "Why do You enclose her, Lord?" Because *a day will come when they will speak to her*, and the greatest work of God will be done when they speak to the Virgin; and a great preparation is necessary for that day. "And what are they adorning her for?" For the wedding day. "She will enter happily, Lord!"

Her parents bring her at three years old, and they set her on the lowest step of the altar, which had fifteen steps by which one could ascend;[329] and she ascended with great litheness. Whether she ascended by a miracle or not, it's not said; piously, it can be believed that such things befell this Girl after she was born, so that all would marvel at her and have their eyes set on her and say, "What's to be done with this Girl?" Because it should be believed that God would

[329] Jewish and Catholic tradition alike state that the Temple in Jerusalem had a set of fifteen steps (the Southern Steps), and that one of the fifteen Songs of Ascent (Psalms 120–135) was sung on each step. The story of the child Mary ascending the fifteen steps is from the *Gospel of Pseudo-Matthew,* a Latin work from around the seventh century. The older, Greek *Protoevangelium of James,* from around the second century—which is the main source for traditions regarding Mary's conception, birth, and childhood—instead says that she was placed on the third step, and there is no mention of ascent. See *Gospel of Pseudo-Matthew*, Ch. IV, and *Protoevangelium of James* VII.2, as found in *The Apocryphal New Testament*, ed. and tr. Montague Rhodes James (Oxford: Clarendon Press, 1975), 73, 42.

always do great marvels for her whom He created as His Mother. She ascends; her parents offer her to God. She enters most happily! Let us offer our hearts with her. The best offering of a pure creature that was ever offered or will be offered was the Virgin. "Freely you give her to Me"—says God—"freely I receive her."[330] The Virgin enters the monastery; she did not enter crying nor unwillingly, nor did what she left behind weigh upon her, although she was a girl; but she said, "Let my eyes not see the things of this world. For love of You, let my mouth be closed; let me keep silence, for I will have to speak of You to You; let me be where all command me, where I will serve all for love of You." Very willingly, she enters to serve God.

This Girl Is Good for a Wall

She having entered the monastery, *what will we do with our sister for the day when they are to speak to her?*[331] What can we do so that God will be enamored of her? What will we do? "*If she is a wall, let us build upon it a silver rampart.*"[332] The same divine word, asking, responds and says: *Since she is a wall, let us build upon her towers of silver.*[333] How do you call her *wall*? What does a girl of three years old have to do with walls? Walls are tall, wide, hard, and deep, and even more if they are like those of the Promised Land, for some spies whom the sons of Israel had sent [there] said: *They have some well-fortified cities, some walls up to heaven.*[334] So God speaks truth, that she is a wall; *so let us build upon her things that shall defend her.*

Higher than heaven, deeper than hell, longer than earth, and wider than sea.[335] This little girl of whom we speak is higher than heaven,

330 Cf. Mt 10:8.

331 Sg 8:8.

332 *"Si murus est, aedificemus super eum propugnacula argentea."* Sg 8:9.

333 *Si murus est, aedificemus,* etc.

334 Dt 3:5.

335 *Excelsior caelo, profundior inferno, longior terra, et latior mari.* Job 11:8–9. These verses were applied to Mary in a Pseudo-Augustinian sermon on the

deeper than the abysses, wider than earth. Higher than heaven in what is spiritual. What is "better" we call "higher" and great. Among all the things God created, except the humanity of Jesus Christ, among all pure creatures, there is none other so excellent, and thus, none as high; for, although she is a little girl, she is more than the angels, more than the seraphim. Blessed be You, Lord, for, from our generation, You gave us this Girl, higher than heaven! If you want her as thoughts, highest; if you want her as foundation, deepest; if you have good eyes, prepare to see this Girl, most humble in her eyes. In this Virgin, there is nothing more excellent than her humility. She well knew the great deeds God did for her, but attributed nothing of the good she had to herself, nor to her powers. There is no pure creature who so truly gives God honor like this Virgin. See if she has good foundations.

Does she lack wideness? This Virgin is a wall for all the whole world, and not only for it, which is little, but also for all men. See how many there are who lived and who died, and others and others came. Finally, we are all sons of Eve according to the flesh, and of the Virgin according to the spirit. This Girl has a Mother's affection, a defender's heart, for all men; see if she needs to be long in order to be the Mother of so many sons. Girl, where do you get your mantle from, in order to cover us all? Where the wings to shelter so many little chicks? She is wider than earth! The just and the sinners fit into her; sinners are pardoned through her pleas, and the just conserved by grace; she fits Him who does not fit into heaven, wider than earth, and heaven, and angels; for since God entered into her and fit into her, will you not fit, sinner? *Holy and immaculate virginity, I do not know what praises to offer you, since Him Whom the heavens could*

Assumption; see *Sermon* 208.4: "But what will we, so small, what will we, little in action, what will we bring to her praises, when, even if all of our members were turned into tongues, naught would suffice to praise her? For higher than heaven is she whom we speak of; deeper than abyss, she to whom we strive to say praises" (PL 39:2130).

not contain, you received in your womb.[336] *He Who does not fit in the heavens was enclosed in your bowels*; well will you fit, sinner, into the bowels of the Virgin.

Blessed be God, who gave us such a Girl as a wall, as Jeremiah said: *Today I have given you as a column of iron and a wall of metal.*[337] She is a wall, but she is not one for those whom God calls easy walls, walls of glass. Who are these? God forbid that the one talking to you be so! Priests, prophets, renowned men, I have a great complaint against you: *that you did not set yourselves up as a wall*[338] for the house of Israel, so that you would be there *on the day of the Lord's battle.*[339] A brave thing! "I walk about"—says God—"seeking a man who will place himself between Me and men, so that, if I want to chastise them, he will be on their side; and, because I did not find him, *I poured forth My indignation.*"[340] When is *the day of the Lord's battle*? When our great sins arise before His justice. God wills that, when He is angry with the people, their priests would go hand-to-hand with Him, so that He would not pour out His wrath. God complains that He is looking for someone to go hand-to-hand with Him, and among so many, He did not find one. Those are walls of glass, those are the ones who do not have justice for us; and if we don't have [justice] to defend ourselves, how will we have it for others? How will we be able to take away God's wrath against His people? The Virgin is not one of those shattered walls nor one of those who cannot suffer a blow for charity towards his neighbor. The most strong girl, raised and hardened in labors, is good for a wall.

---

336 *Sancta et immaculata virginitas, quibus te laudibus efferam nescio, quia quem caeli capere non poterant, tuo gremio contulisti.* From the responsory to the first reading at Matins for the Common of the Blessed Virgin Mary.

337 Jer 1:18.

338 *Quia non opposuistis vos murum.*

339 Ez 13:5.

340 *Effudi indignationem.* Jer 10:25.

The Arms of the Virgin, Love and Recollection

What arms could we have for fighting with the Lord, so to conquer Him? Happily the Girl enters! What are you carrying, Lady? You are carrying a great task: to fight with God, so that He will love men; may the Lord give you arms. What arms are you carrying? Are they riches? No, for she has left them all behind; and, when she was grown-up, she labored with her hands for food. Then, what are you carrying? Beauty? She knew what the Wise Man says, *that grace is deceiving and beauty vain.*[341] So she is not like that. Then, what are you carrying to conquer? Let Him say it: *You have wounded My heart with one of your eyes and with one hair of your head.*[342] Her great love, her great obedience and virtues wounded the Lord. On the days of Our Lady, we have to confess and commune and give many praises to Our Lady, as a sign that, on those days, God does mercies through her pleas. Don't you believe that, for those who prepare themselves on these days, God will do them great mercies, since He loves this blessed Lady Virgin so much?

What will we put on the Girl? What arms will we give her to fight against God, and even to conquer Him? *You have wounded My heart, My bride, with one of your eyes and with one hair of your head.* Blessed be You, Lord! Are You so tender that You are wounded upon seeing them, and so weak that You are tied up with one hair? What do You mean to tell us, Lord, except that You have arms and heart ready to receive us? What is more tender than to be wounded by sight? Here you see the arms with which the Virgin fights. What will this one eye—not two—be? *Incline your ear,* says God.[343] Not two ears; it is no more than one. *One thing is necessary,*[344] one love, one unmixed intention. This is the eye of which the Lord spoke in another place:

---

341 Prv 31:30.

342 *Vulnerasti cor meum in uno oculorum tuorum, et in uno crine colli tui.* Sg 4:9.

343 Ps 45:10.

344 *Unum est necessarium.* Lk 10:42.

If your eye be simple, all your body will be resplendent.[345] Oh sorrow: how far away was the heart of the Girl from those who said: *Your wine has been mixed with water, and your gold has turned to dross!*[346] The *wine* of the Virgin is her intention; an eye untwisted, unmixed. She did not will that her will be done, but God's. "Let Your will be done; let it not be done according to me, but You; let me see Your will fulfilled." The Virgin loves God and herself for God and the profit of men. This was the eye of the Virgin, a clear eye; he who loves God will love his neighbor well. *You have wounded Me with one of your eyes.* There is nothing with which one more easily attains God than with love; God doesn't know how to defend himself against the heart that loves Him, because He doesn't want to. There is no crossbow that wounds so quickly. A Girl, and such love! Christ says: *Where your treasure is, there is your heart.*[347] If the eye is right, the head is no more than one; because, if the intention is right towards God, there is no more than one thought; everything is employed upon God. What is your treasure like? A treasure of muck and coals if you've placed it on earth, flesh and vanity, or in the wind of honor: ruined treasure! Where what you love is, there is your heart.

"What will I do, Father, since I feel like praying, and I'm dry as straw, without devotion?" Brother, see how much what you love affects your heart; place your treasure in heaven, and your heart will go towards what you love. If love is mucky, how will you have a tranquil heart?

The Girl, a love! Who would see you sing the psalms with greater spirit than David himself, who composed them! *What do I have*, Lord, *in heaven?*[348] *And, besides You, what do I want upon earth? God is my portion!*[349] One thing God wants, that my portion

---

345 Mt 6:23.

346 Is 1:22.

347 Mt 6:21.

348 *Quid mihi est in caelo?*

349 Ps 73:25–26.

be pure love; and, because you had no more than one God, you had no more than one love. Of God she thought when she ate and when she talked; wherever she walked, she always walked thinking of God. The angels, admiring this, said: *Who is this who ascends from the desert?*[350] Lord, shame befalls me in saying these words; but this shame is removed upon seeing that she, who prayed so well, is flesh of our flesh. *Who is this who arises from the desert like a little rod of smoke?*[351] What will the prayer of the Virgin be like, since the angels marvel at it? *Who is this who arises like smoke?* Smoke, not from green wood nor which makes one cry, like that of our [prayer], for we ask for vengeance upon our enemies, and for earthly things; that is smoke which makes one cry; it is not a rod that rises up, but rather, since it is earth, it remains on earth.

Then, what is the Virgin's [prayer] like? *Of aromatics, of myrrh.*[352] Smoke of frankincense, of benzoin, and of storax,[353] and of fragrant fruit: such were the thoughts of the Virgin. Saint Bernard: "Some have the act of prayer, and not the life of men who pray."[354] From all this sweet-smelling powder,[355] there will be good prayer, accompanied by good works of charity, of fasting, and of disciplines.[356] For what profit is it to weep a little, if the rest is talking? What does it profit you to have a bit of prayer at night, if you waste the day in laughter and vanities? That is not the life of a man who prays, because he who will truly pray has to keep himself, all day long, from offending God, and he has to walk about always asking God Our Lord: "Give me more knowledge of You!" Because when will

---

350 *Quae est ista, quae ascendit de deserto?* Sg 8:5.

351 Sg 3:6.

352 *Ex aromatibus myrrhae.* Sg 3:6.

353 These are all different types of resins that are burned for fragrance, like incense.

354 Unfortunately, we have not been able to locate the source of this quotation.

355 Cf. Sg 3:6.

356 A "discipline," in this context, is an ascetic or penitential practice, such as the wearing of a hairshirt.

you be rich if you don't join the penny[357] of today with that of tomorrow and of yesterday, and guard it very well?

From this, it comes about that so few men profit in the spirit during so much time. And the same Saint Bernard says: "You will find more people who turn from evil to good than from good to better."[358] It seems to us that we are secure when we do not commit mortal sins; God wakes us so that we might serve Him, and He has not finished waking us, when we turn back to sleeping and falling into our flimsiness. The Virgin had prayer and a life conforming to it, because what comes out of a careless heart goes down. Since the Virgin has her thought so recollected, she is good for fighting, since she has arms for conquering God; now, let us enter into the fight.

The Virgin Conquers God in Prayer

He who wants to see jousts and the running of bulls, let him see it in good time. He who wants to see great squadrons of people and blood spilling out, let him see it; to my eyes, nothing else seems good but that war: to see a Girl of three years, on the one side, a cloistered maiden, and on the other, God. Oh, so blessed a game! And who would see the Girl fight with God, more tired than the patriarch Jacob! But he fought for no more than one night, and with an angel; but he did it wisely, for, since he had to fight, he cast his women, and shepherds, and gains, and beasts

---

357 In Spanish, *blanca*, a small billon coin whose value and silver content kept shrinking throughout the centuries. In St. John's time, 68 *blancas* could be exchanged for one *real*. Its meager value inspired idioms like "to have not even a *blanca*" (*no tener ni blanca*) or "to be without a *blanca*" (*estar sin blanca*) to express absolute poverty.

358 See St. Bernard, *Epistle* 96: "This is the finger of God, subtly working, sweetly renewing, profitably changing, making, not only good men from bad, but better from good . . . You will much more easily find many secular men converted to the good than any one man among the religious passing on to the better" (PL 182:229B).

up ahead; he made them pass the river, and he alone remained on the other side, prepared to fight well.[359] Do you want to pray well? Cast ahead of you all that impedes you; tell all your affairs, "Depart from me, for I am going to deal with God!" And if it is contempt for someone, when a king or lord is standing there talking to him, to turn back to other things, what will it be when one, while standing there talking to God, wanders about hither and thither in his thoughts? Jacob fought for one night alone, and alone; the Virgin fought, her heart more recollected. Jacob fought prepared, but the Virgin more prepared. And so, the Bridegroom says: *A closed garden, my bride, my friend, a closed garden*:[360] the body enclosed in the monastery, the eyes and ears enclosed, and the thoughts enclosed within herself.

Who would see the Girl arise in the dark of night and sit herself in a little corner and begin to battle God with her heart! *Lord, if I have found grace in Your eyes, forgive them.*[361] Yes, for so Moses prayed; but how does prayer compare with prayer? Good was Moses's, better the Virgin's. "*Lord, if I have found grace before You,* do this mercy towards men, cure the souls that are lost. *Let the Lamb come*, Lord, let the *desired of the nations* come.[362] Cure us, Lord; let the water which impregnates the earth come."[363] The Virgin begged the Lord that He would send His Son to be served by her who was His Mother; she wanted to be a servant, and she was the Mother. Who would see what a response God gave her!

A worm you are, an ant you are, who wander about the earth, and the Virgin is pleading for you in heaven: "Lord, mercy for the one who called upon me, and mercy for the one who commended himself to me."

---

[359] Gn 32:13–21.

[360] *Hortus conclusus.* Sg 4:12.

[361] *Domine, si inveni gratiam in oculis tuis, dimitte eis.* Ex 34:9.

[362] Is 16:1; Hag 2:8 (Vulgate).

[363] See Is 45:8.

"Do you not see that he has committed such sin and deserves punishment?" That is the blow: "That man does not deserve mercy." Those are the blows that the justice of God gives to the one who sets herself to pleading for another.

"Who would see you respond! What reply do you have?"

"Lord, do I come before You to claim justice or to ask for mercy? Well do I see that he deserves punishment; but I ask You for mercy, Lord; either *erase me from the book of life or pardon* this one."[364] If Moses had the charity to ask this of God, will not the Virgin have it? "Let the curse of the penalty come upon me, and Your blessing upon them; I offer You my life and salvation; punish me, and pardon them; I offer You my honor: treat me as You will, and be pious to these pious bowels."[365] Will I not believe this of your bowels, since you have more pious ones than Moses's, and he asked this of God? Will I not believe, Lady, that you will take pity on sinners, since God created you for them? A thousand times the Virgin offered her life for men. If we walked with mouth on the ground for love of her, it would be little; if we loved her and poured out our blood for her, and lost our life for her, it would be little. What do you offer, Lady, for men? Your life? It is little: she offered another life, which she loved much more than her own. May men give you thanks! She knew that the will of God, in order for the world to be healed, was that the Son would die. "May my Son die, since You, Father, will it!" How much you will feel, with a Mother's sorrow! "Let Your will be done, Lord." How much we owe you! He who could reckon how much the Virgin loved Jesus Christ, he could reckon how much we owe her.

Thus the Virgin prayed to the Lord: "Lord, if the world deserves punishment, let it come upon me, and do mercy to them." Saint

---

364 Ex 32:32.

365 Recall what was mentioned in footnote 290 in the previous sermon; that many languages consider the bowels, or the entrails, the seat of deep emotion and compassion.

Bernard says: *Tepid is every prayer which inspiration does not precede.*[366] There are many testimonies of this here; cold is every prayer when the inspiration of the Holy Spirit does not move it; one prays coldly when the holy sigh does not come first. Saint Paul: *The Spirit pleads for us with groans that cannot be counted.*[367] And Saint Paul, another time: *The Holy Spirit, Who is within us, teaches us to pray.*[368] He often makes our hearts explode, for many times man does not know why he weeps. *The Holy Spirit pleads with groans that cannot be counted*, nor does the very man who gives [the groans] understand them. It doesn't matter at all that you don't understand them, for that God who inspires them in us understands them and makes you plead in conformity with what He wills. How great will your prayers be, Virgin, since they were moved by the Holy Spirit!

Then if the same God taught her to pray, it is clear that He would hear the prayers of the Virgin. She won more from God than Jacob did, more than Moses did. What does Moses ask of God? "Lord, that You would hold Your hands back; that You would not punish this people." Finally, at that time, he raised his hands to God so that He would not punish his people, and the Virgin raises her hands to Him with her prayers so that He will remove His wrath and anger from men. A holy man, how much he wins from God! If he wants to take away the world's hunger, he says to Him: "Lord, I beseech You, do not send hunger upon the world, through Your mercy. What [hunger] there is, with its sufferings, remove them from us, Lord, remove those pains." Lady, what will you win? "Lord, may You take away sufferings!" She wins it that God would take on pains and sufferings for men. To the rush of the Virgin's prayers, God responds. She brings Him from the heavens to earth, He enters into her womb, she arms Him with some arms and so delicate a flesh that hunger and thirst and tiredness fatigue it, and thorns prick it, giving

---

366 *Tepida est omnis oratio, quam non praecedit inspiration.* See St. Bernard, *On Loving God* VII.22 (PL 182:987D).

367 Rom 8:26.

368 See Rom 8:26.

it five thousand and odd lashes; and He holds back His hands, and He is silent, and they stuff Him with sufferings, and He says to the Father: *Pardon them, Lord*![369] Who can win so great a thing from God? Through the prayers of the Virgin. God says: *Woman, great is your faith; let it be done as you will.*[370] *If you were strong against God, how much more against men*?[371] Jacob went forth, fearful of his brother Esau. Jacob, you had fought with the Lord, *strong against God, how much more* will you be so *against* your brother? Virgin, who could stand before your power? Who will you not conquer, since you have conquered God? It is because of this that the demons tremble at the Virgin, fleeing her when she is named; her name is frightful against them. The one persecuted by the demon runs back to the Virgin with faith, for, later, he will be freed of it. One of the principal remedies against the demon is to run back to the Virgin.

The Humility of Mary!

Why are you frightened [at the fact] that, being with those maidens, she prevails over them all and reigns over them? She who poured forth such tears, what conversation do you think she'll have? What joy will she show on her face, as you see, even here, on the face of a man when he leaves prayer? Brides of Christ, devotees of the Virgin, no one has seen the Virgin angry. And, although she does not show anger on her face, do not think that she went into a corner to get angry, so that, although she disguised it on the outside, she had anger in her heart. *Learn from Me*—says the Lord—*for I am meek and humble of heart.*[372] Such was the Virgin: meek, soft towards all, seeking the last place; she wouldn't be an abbess! May God give us His grace so that we might understand this.

---

369 Lk 23:34.

370 Mt 15:28.

371 *Si contra Deum fortis fuisti, quanto magis contra homines*? Gn 32:28.

372 Mt 11:29.

They beg the Son to be king; He does not want it, and He goes away, fleeing; they did not find Him. "Why don't You want to be king? Could they, perhaps, deceive You, or would You twist justice? Why don't You want it? Will You, perhaps, fall into sin?"

No.

"Then why do You flee from so secure a thing?" The Lord flees from dignities in order to make us understand that, if He who was so secure fled, then the unfortunate worm should flee such occasions. The sick man who pretends himself healthy—"neither sun nor air will do me ill; well can I eat what I want, for I'm already well"—the sick man who wants to be treated as healthy will quickly fall again, and experience will make him understand that he was sick and not healthy. *A most hard sentence*—says God—*will be given those who hold command*,[373] so much more so if they are given money for it.

"Sell me your regiment, your twenty-four men." Madman! Where are your eyes? You see a tiny speck on your vine and on your olive tree, you keep such an account of your funds, and, in your health, you have such vigilance that you walk about, looking out, [saying] "this will harm me, that will profit me," even in very trifling things, and [do you have] so much carelessness in what touches your soul? You see a little speck, and you do not see a very great mountain! It is a shame to see some men, so astute in hair-splitting things and so foolish in things that matter so much. What is more foolish than saying, "Take my money so that God will judge me with a hard sentence"? Because what does it mean to say, "Sell me your twenty-four men," except, in plain language [to say], "Take a thousand ducats so that you'll give me what will send me to hell"? Are you not content—woe is you!—with a *hard* sentence, but at your own cost, you instead want to buy a *most hard sentence*, since you are taking an office you don't deserve?

The Virgin suffered persecutions; but it is written of her that she was joyful in persecutions. A Virgin with such light in her

---

373 Ws 6:5.

understanding, such force in her will, such humility: How bad would be it for you to show yourself in the world, Virgin, since you are so secure against falling? You might perform a miracle. Saints who are as far from the Virgin as heaven from earth perform miracles: so many miracles for little bitty saints, none for Your Mother? I suspect the Virgin cast herself at the feet of her Son, because, in this life, she does nothing for herself, due to the greatness of the humility she had. She begged this of her Son: "Let them not know me, let nothing be done which would resound to my glory or honor." Well do you know our weakness, for we are friends of our own harm, of high places. "Let me be, for I have to be a model for the many people who will come after me; I have to be an example to married women, to widows and maidens, to give them an example, so that they might love the last place; although it could be done to me safely,[374] I don't want it." The humility of the Virgin, *the slave of the Lord*![375] And so I believe that she was the first in obeying, and that she took up the broom for sweeping, and that she always did the lowest tasks.

Oh, who would see this Virgin as she dealt with those whom she had in her company? How many maidens came to this maiden when they were disconsolate! When someone was disconsolate and came to her, how she prayed to God: "Lord, healing! Let not this disconsolate women come to me in vain!" Who came to you without receiving this good from Him? It is not surprising that she who was strong with God was so with men, and thus I believe that she took the hearts of all captive. Taken from the monastery, they marry her off; married, she lived a virgin all her days. Do you believe that, when she lived in the monastery of virgins, they loved her well? Do you believe that she gained mercies from God for them? It is to be believed, then, that, being so far from us, there are so many who love her well.

---

374 That is, her humility is such that she could not fall victim to pride, no matter how much glory or honor she received.

375 Lk 1:38.

A Sign of Predestination: Having a Great Devotion for the Virgin

I ask you: Why do you say to me, "How many Christian hearts are there today who would suffer death for the Virgin's honor!"? This is true! What is this? How do we love the Virgin so much? How are there so many people who love her and who hold Mary written in their hearts? Lady, if your virtues could snatch the heart of God, how much more could they snatch the [heart] of men! Your neck is the Church, like the *tower of David, a thousand shields hang from it, all the arms of the strong.*[376] "Who is the head?" Christ. "Who the neck?" She who joins, with her prayers, the body to the head, mediatrix between God and men, higher than anyone; both near God, in goodness and height, and near us, by mercy; higher than anyone, but lower than all in her own eyes. The Virgin's neck is a tower: *your neck is like an ivory tower.*[377] On that neck, *a thousand shields hang,* where the strong are armed and weak are welcomed into it.

What a thing, what a thing! How many maidens have there been whom the world plied with rich marriages and states, and over how many of them did the love of the Virgin prevail, so that they would cast all this away and say: "For love of the Virgin, I promise virginity to God and to her!" *Virgins will be drawn to the King after her.*[378] In good time was she a virgin, and in good time did she enter the monastery! *Many virgins will be drawn to the King after her*, for love of her, through wanting to follow her virginity. He who wages war with his flesh knows that in her *the strong are armed*, and that he will conquer [the flesh] with love of the Virgin.

If you are too weak to fast during vigils, may you become strong. How many martyrs, through the strength of this martyr, became martyrs, remembering the suffering that she had before the Cross,

---

376 *Turris David, mille clypei pendent ex ea, omnis armatura fortium.* Sg 4:4.

377 *Collum tuum sicut turris eburnea.* Sg 7:4.

378 *Adducentur Regi virgines post eam.* Ps 45:14.

and said, "I want to have patience in my labor, since this Virgin had so much in hers!" How many mothers were consoled for the loss of their children by remembering the Son whom this Virgin saw die before her eyes! And how many poor men were consoled by her poverty and labors! How many pardoned offenses done to them because the Virgin pardoned the one who killed her Son! For suffering and pardoning and being virgins, there is an example in the Virgin.

Lady, and we, the weak, will we not find some remedy for our weakness in you? If the flesh holds you back, call to Mary. Blessed be God! Haven't you ever seen this marvel: a man and a woman who have such virtue that, the more you love them, the more chaste you are? Who put chastity into the heart of a man who greatly loves a woman? So you see here a Virgin who, the more a man is enamored of her, the more chaste he will be. God gave one virginal flesh to Jesus Christ and to the Virgin (for all is one), which is enough to sanctify other flesh. The woman who is enamored of Jesus Christ will be more chaste by it, and the more she is enamored of Him, the more chaste she will be.

The only remedy against the temptations of the flesh is to receive the body of Jesus Christ with purity. You'll tell me: "The weak and persons who often receive the Lord, why aren't they chaste?" Because they don't receive the body of Jesus Christ well; because, if they received [His body] well, they wouldn't stop being firm in purity. From Adam, the filthiness of his flesh came to us; yet purer is the flesh of Jesus Christ than that of Adam was filthy; and if we receive [His body] well, [He] will purify us more than the other one dirtied us, unless we receive [Him] badly.

"What will I do, since I am tempted by the flesh?" Hold on to the Virgin as an advocate, for she smells very greatly of incense, since *in the plazas she poured out her scent.*[379] The Virgin smells of myrrh which kills worms, which signifies chastity, which kills the worms

[379] Sir 24:19–20.

of filthiness;[380] because, if you were devoted to her, you would feel temptations come undone, like wax *before the fire.*[381] Call upon the Virgin and tell her: "Lady, because I do you service, I will fight with love against love: with your [love] against the love of my evil flesh."

And the Virgin has arms for the weak and those tempted by desperation. Saint Bernard: "In all your necessities and labors, call upon Mary, for, if she was powerful against God, will she not be powerful against your enemies? And if you walk through the tempestuous sea of this world, look to the north, look to Mary; let him alone not call her who called her in his necessities, with all his heart, and she did not succor him."[382]

Do you think that being devoted to the Virgin is taking off your hat when the name "Mary" is said, and nothing more? One's devotion needs to have deeper roots, for so says our Redeemer: *Send*

---

380 Medically, myrrh has long been used as a remedy against parasites, especially intestinal worms.

381 Ps 68:2.

382 St. Bernard, *On the Words of the Gospel: "The Angel Gabriel Was Sent"*, II.17: "Then, at the end of the verse, it says, *And the name of the Virgin was Mary.* Let's talk a little also about this name, which is said to mean *star of the sea [maris stella]*, and is very conveniently befitting to the Virgin mother . . . O, whoever among you feels, in the current of this world, that he is being more tossed about among storms and tempests than walking on earth, do not avert your eyes from the blaze of this star, if you don't want to be overwhelmed by storms. If the winds of temptations rise up, if you run into the cliffs of tribulations, look at the star, call upon Mary. If you are thrown into the waves of pride, of ambition, of detraction, of emulation, look to the star, call upon Mary. If the lures of wrath or greed or the flesh bash against the little boat of your mind, look to Mary. If, disturbed by the immensity of your crimes, confused by the ugliness of your conscience, terrified by horror of judgment, you begin to be swallowed up by the pit of the abyss, think of Mary. In dangers, in anguishes, in doubtful things, think of Mary, call upon Mary. Let her not recede from your mouth, let her not recede from your heart; and, as you implore the succor of her prayer, do not desert the example of her way of life. Following her, you will not go awry; begging her, you will not despair; thinking of her, you will not go astray" (PL 183:70C–71A). This set of sermons is often known by its short Latin name: *Super "Missus est."*

out roots among My elect.[383] "What roots?" A great devotion of the heart towards the Virgin; and he who does not have it, let him not rest until he finds it. One of the signs of those who are to be saved is having a great devotion for the Virgin. *Cast forth roots*, Mother, *among My elect.* "How will I gain this devotion?" How did her parents, who were so sterile, gain her from God? Your heart is as sterile as her parents were for gaining such a Daughter. Then, how did they do it? With fasting and tears, with prayers, and keeping the law of God very closely; and, in payment for this, God gave them Mary. "What do I have to do in order to have devotion for the Virgin?" You don't have devotion for her? You're in a really bad state; you're missing quite a lot; it would be much better to be without skin than to be without devotion to Mary. *Cast forth roots among My elect.* "What should I do to attain this?" Give alms. When you see your neighbor's daughter who, due to necessity, is going to be lost, say: "I want to make this maiden a nun or marry her off for love of the Virgin. I want to fast for her on Saturdays, keep vigils, stick to bread and water," or whatever you can do; "I want to pray this Rosary for love of her." For such is the love of this Lady that, even if you pour out your blood, it is well-employed for her.

Keep the Son before His Father, and the Mother before her Son. Offer the Son to the Father, and say: "Lord, I offer You what You gave me; by His wounds, have compassion on me, Lord." If you have devotion to those wounds and offer them to His Father with faith that He will hear you, you have a great good. Because, if you do not take advantage of Jesus Christ and of His labors, it will be considered a great ingratitude in you; for the benefits made to the ungrateful are counted as lost. God died for you, and you do not feel it and do not take advantage of it; on your side, it's just as if He hadn't died; rather, it will be of great harm to you, for your labors will be very terribly demanded of you; instead, say, "Father, I owe You much; for Your Son's sake, do me this mercy."

---

[383] *In electis meis mitte radices.* Sir 24:13.

Just as the Father gave us a most great gift in giving us His blessed Son for our remedy, so, too, the Son gave us a great gift in giving us His blessed Mother as our advocate. I know that when the Son told Saint John, at the foot of the Cross, *behold your mother*,[384] He spoke in the name of all: all of us Christians enter there. God gives us His Mother as mother; let us thank Him, and let the angels thank Him. If you do this, if you place the Son before the Father and the Mother before the Son, you have a great sign of salvation.

What Will I Do for the Virgin?

"What will I do for the Virgin? God has given me many goods through her; what will I do for her?" Do you remember the wedding feast when the wine failed, and the Virgin told her Son, "Son, *they have no wine*; I have compassion for them"? Our Redeemer told her: *Woman, what do I have to do with you?* "I understand it well!" She goes to those who serve the wedding feast: *all that* my Son *tells you, do it.*[385] What a brief speech, but how chock-full! Here she preached as much as Isaiah, Saint Paul, and Saint Luke, and all the apostles and prophets. *Now, sons, listen to me*;[386] *listen to me*, to what I want to tell you; perhaps, from the mouth of the Mother, it will be imprinted on your hearts; *All that my Son tells you, do it.* And so the greatest service you can do is to do what her Son commands: "Lady, for love of you, I pardon this injury." Do you have wicked love for a woman? "I want to separate myself from her for your sake. I want to be silent, I want to keep silence for love of you; what it hurts me most to do or to stop doing, I offer it for the Virgin." To love her well and to not imitate her profits little. Let us imitate her in humility and in the other virtues, because she is the model from whom we need to draw them, and doing this will gain us grace and later glory.

384 Jn 19:27.

385 *Quodqumque dixerit vobis, facite.* Jn 2:3–5.

386 *Nunc, filii, audite me.* Prv 8:32.

Sermon 78

He Who Loves Me, Let Him Deny Himself

(October 4: St. Francis of Assisi, Gal 6:14–18; Mt 11:25–30)
Given in a convent of nuns

"Venite ad me omnes qui laboratis et onerati estis, et ego reficiam vos."
"Come to Me, all you who labor and are burdened, and I will refresh you."[387]

Exordium

I WILL confess You, Lord, Father of heaven and earth, for You have hidden these things from the wise and prudent, and have revealed them to the little.[388] So begins the most holy Gospel of today's Mass. *I praise You, Lord, Father of heaven and earth, for You have hidden these things from the wise and prudent and revealed them to the little children.* What things did God hide from the wise and prudent and reveal to the little children? Many things, and one of them is what He revealed to this holy blessed one, Saint Francis. He revealed this secret to him: that He had made him a friend of begging, of asking for the love of God. There has never been someone who has been

---

[387] Mt 11:28.

[388] *Confitebor tibi Domine, Pater caeli et terrae, quia abscondisti haec a sapientibus et prudentibus, et revelasti ea parvulis.* Mt 11:25.

such a friend of poverty. God revealed to him that this—begging—was a great art for acquiring great riches, and it was not such so much for the body as for the soul; and, if we look at this well, there is no day in which we do not come to the door of God to beg, saying, "Lord, give us bread; bread, Lord." *Give us this day our daily bread.*[389]

This saint was so founded on the knowledge of himself, and this is not little: you don't have this even a little, for God gives it to few. It is said of him that, in the prayer he made, God revealed two things to him, revealed two abysses to him: The one, that of his own poverty and weakness. The other, [that of] the great riches of God. If you see this, and God reveals it to you, you will say, "Lord, there is nothing so befitting to me as You. How well Your mercy goes with my misery, Your wisdom with my foolishness, Your riches with my poverty! You and I, Lord, we have been well-matched, and You fit me well." Saint Francis, seeing this, said, "Lord, and Who are you, and who am I?" Because of this, he came to distance himself from himself, to distrust his own powers; this begging, too, came to him, this walking about laden with God, and this walking about to ask for God's sake; and so he said that he wanted his friars to pray rather than study. He became poor; God helped him. He walked about begging; he was enriched. This is the secret that God reveals to the one who distrusts himself. This is the secret attained by those who do not lean upon their own powers, the little low ones, and these are those who also attain this secret: *Ask and it will be given you; call, and it will be given you.*[390] Asking Him like little low ones, like little children, as a little poor man asks a rich man, who does nothing but show him his wounds, reveal his needs to him.

And so, He commands us, in the words of the theme, that we should go to Him, and that He will heal us, and we cannot [do so] without His grace and aid, as we say; let us ask for it, and let us make the Most Holy Virgin Mary, Our Lady, our intercessor.

---

389 *Panem nostrum*, etc.

390 Mt 7:7.

This Rest Is with a Condition: Deny Yourself

Come to Me, all you who labor and are burdened, and I will refresh you.[391] If the sermon that's preached today were of the same flavor as the words of the theme, we would all go away consoled. But, in the end, when the meal is good, even if it wasn't so well stewed, it doesn't lose its flavor because [of] this. God says—and He alone can say it—*Come to Me, you who are labored, for I will give you rest.* (Certainly, at His own cost). "Although it costs Me much, I will give you rest." (That is charity: to labor for another's rest). *Come to Me, all of you.* Who, Lord, and from where to where? All of you who are in very deep labors, in great miseries, you who are separated from all rest (since it comes from Me): whatever the labor you have, whatever the load that weighs you down, *come to Me, for I will unburden you* and refresh you. I will remedy your needs; I will satisfy your hunger; come to Me. Certainly, this is a great invitation, Christ inviting us and calling us from such labor to such rest. It is a great invitation.

Look now: I find a difficulty in this. Who is there in the world who would not willingly accept this invitation? Who is there who, if he is laboring, does not desire to rest? I said: Why are you going to the Indies? To get money, for what you need in order to rest; because you think about how you will rest when you don't lack it. Why are you busy? To gain health, because you think that, having it, you will rest. Yes, you labor and die in order to find rest. Ah, Lord! We will give as much as we have for a little bit of rest; we wander about seeking it through some ways and through others; and Jesus Christ says that we should go to Him, that He will give it to us. Why don't we go? For, if He invites us, why don't we go?

Look now: if it were no more than this, there would be no one, small or great, evil or good, who would not go after Jesus Christ and accept the invitation that He makes, to rest from their labors. But

---

[391] *Venite ad me omnes qui laboratis et onerati estis et ego reficiam vos.* Mt 11:28.

God cast aloe[392] into this rest, saying a word that He said elsewhere, which seems to fit well here, with a condition. He said: "The Son of the Virgin will be dishonored, lashed, crucified, and He will die".

Saint Peter took this and said to Him: "Lord, You lashed? You dead? God shall never want that.[393] Do not say such a thing, Lord."

"What are you saying, Saint Peter? Are you giving Me counsel—*Me*—about what I should do? *Not those things which are God's, but those which are men's.*[394] Walk away, Peter, for you don't know what you're saying. *You do not understand the things of God.* Walk away, since you're speaking like a man. Men are terrified of being someone lashed, crowned, burnt, dishonored, beaten, and despised by all; but God's business isn't like this. You don't want to see them dishonor your Master and lash Him and put Him on a Cross like an evildoer, but rather [you want] them all to hold Him in high esteem, all to honor and serve Him. What thing is this, that He won't suffer this? For, yes, He will suffer all that I say. And since it frightens you to hear that all this is going to happen to Me, it will frighten you more when I tell you that they will lash you, that they will chase you from place to place, dragging you from judge to judge, and that, at the end, they will kill you. It will frighten you more to hear that these things will happen in your own house than to hear that they will happen in another's house: that doesn't frighten you as much. So I advise you that he who would follow Me will suffer all this himself. *If someone wants to come after Me, let him deny himself, take up his cross, and follow Me.*"[395]

Here you see the condition. There he says: *Come to me, you who are labored, for I will give you rest.* Here he says: *If someone wants to come in My footsteps, let him deny himself and take up his cross and follow me.* Here you see the aloe: "He who loves Me, *let him deny himself.*"

---

[392] Connoted here is the bitter flavor of aloe, rather than its soothing properties in soaps and lotions.

[393] See Mt 16:22.

[394] *Non ea quae Dei sunt, sed ea quae hominum.* Mt 16:23.

[395] *abneget semetipsum et tollat crucem suam et sequatur me.* Mt 16:24.

Flavorful, sweet, and smooth is Christ. There is no one who does not delight in following Him, in going to Him; but that bone is very hard to gnaw. Many give up going to Him through His telling them, very loudly: *Let him deny himself.* And let it not seem easy to you that one of the loudest words that Jesus Christ spoke is this; and what makes us know our misery better makes us to understand who we are.

"Lord, he who follows You, how will he follow You?"

"He who loves Me, let him deny himself."

"Lord, if I abandon myself, how will I go after You? How is it that I cannot go after You while carrying myself with me? Don't we fit in one sack, You and I? How is this? There are two: I have to leave the one and have to take up the other. This is a tough thing, that there is so little friendship between You and I, Lord. Has it gone so badly with You and I, Lord, that we don't mesh well together? That, if I would love You, I have to give up myself? How is it that, if I am to follow You, I won't carry myself along? Does it have to be so bad for us? Do we have such a bad condition that we don't fit into one sack, God and us? Lord, don't [we] fit into one sack?"

Your rest and Jesus Christ's labor, your dishonesty and His honesty, your pride and His humility, your wrath and His meekness, your incontinence and His temperance, your lechery and His chastity, do not fit. What you are cannot follow Jesus Christ, if you don't abandon it. For so good is He, and He has no fault: we must be the evil ones. Through our fault, we do not fit, and through our failings. A tough thing You ask of us, Lord: that we would abandon ourselves, that we would deny and again deny ourselves.

Deny Yourself: Abandon Your Own Knowledge and Opinion

"How will this be? How to understand [those words], *he who wants to follow Me, let him deny himself*?" Do you know what you're trying to say? That the old Adam whom we have, whose sons we are, according to the body; that that so-and-so who you are, that you who were born from father and mother, that old man—that is what you have to abandon. If you do not deny that 'you,' you will not be given the grace through which you will be [a son] of God. Who is that you? That man who is not reborn by the Holy Spirit, who is not denied in accord with the will of God, who does not live by the mind[396] of God. Go through those plazas, and you will find three hundred thousand of these; and how many ruled by the opinion of God will you find? That old wisdom, that old reasoning, that old wanting to [be] led by your own will, that old opinion, that "I want this" and "I don't want that," has to be abandoned. It has to be abandoned. That tower of Babylon and that proud Goliath have to be torn down if you are to follow Jesus Christ.

"Tell me, Father." Blessed be You, Lord, Father of heavens and earth, *for You have hidden these things from the wise and prudent and have revealed them to the little children.*[397] Who is that "I" that I have to deny? That being prudent, that wisdom, that thinking that you know what fulfills you, that thinking that you are very lettered and that you, yourselves, know all of this: you have to abandon that. Although, in making shoes, or doing something, or in whatever other office, yes, although it's allowed there; yet, in things that touch your salvation, that business of going to heaven, in how you are in the grace of God, how you fast, how you pray, you cannot know. You have to abandon your knowledge; in everything that relates to serving God, don't think that you know it; you have to deny your knowledge in order to understand it. There is no means by which God reveals Himself to you and teaches you what it means to have love for God and for neighbors, and by which He teaches you what it means to speak of the things of God, except denying your knowledge and casting yourself upon the knowledge of God. To think

---

396 *Seso* means "brain" in modern Spanish, but its older meaning was "the sensitive faculty of the soul" or "opinion."

397 Mt 11:25.

that you don't know what fulfills you, but rather to place yourself entirely in the hands of God. You think it's no more than talk. Woe to you, *not understanding what they say, nor the things they affirm.*[398] We speak, and *we do not understand* what we say *nor the things that we affirm.* How many times do we speak of the love of God, without knowing what it is! How many times do we speak of humility, without having it nor knowing what it is! We cannot appreciate nor hold to those things in what they are, because, as the Apostle says, *the animal man does not perceive those things which are of the spirit of God; for they are foolishness to him.*[399] What is charity, humility, meekness, and all the things which are of the spirit of God? The animal man, without God, does not understand them; all that is a gift and fruit of the Holy Spirit, the animal man does not grasp it, unless aided by the same spirit of God.

"What is that which the Apostle calls *animal man*?" What today's Gospel calls *wise and prudent. I give You thanks, Lord, Father of heaven and earth, for You have hidden these things from the wise and prudent.*[400] Saint Paul, then, calls those men "animals." That is what Plato, on the one hand, and Aristotle, on the other, are; and let them know as much as they want, so much that the common man is terrified of hearing them speak. [Yet,] if God does not teach them, they are animals. *Animal enim voco qui utitur ratione*, says Saint Jerome: "I call 'animal' that which is guided by reason."[401] For that is what he means to call all those who speak of this Christianity and do not follow it. Behold, speaking as men, no one should be called *animal man* except he who is ruled by his appetite, through

---

[398] *Non intelligentes quae loquuntur, neque de quibus affirmant.* 1 Tm 1:7.

[399] *Animal homo non percipit ea quae sunt spiritus Dei; stultitia enim est illi.* 1 Cor 2:14.

[400] Mt 11:25.

[401] I have not found anywhere where St. Jerome uses this line; the closest is where he says, "man, rational animal, adored copper and stone" (*Commentary on Isaiah* I, PL 24:49D). This is simply echoing Aristotle's philosophical definition of man. St. John interprets the phrase in quite a different way.

which we belong with the beasts; because, if you do what a beast does, let them call you "animal." If you are enraged whenever you want something, what more does a beast do in lashing out when it's opposed? If you follow your flesh in all that it asks of you; if, when you fancy being evil to someone, you are so; if, when you fancy sins of the flesh, you later act upon it; if you understand nothing but eating and drinking and sleeping, [nothing] but walking about wrapped up in filthy delights and guiding yourself by what your bestial appetite wants, where is the human being, tell me? Truly, let them call you "beast" and "animal." But, so that they won't call you a beast among men, let them call you a man who is led by reason. Thus you have to live by reason so that they won't call you a beast.

He who was honored there is dishonored here, in regards to God; he who is held to be wise there is, here, held to be a fool; he who is held there to be prudent and someone who knows what fulfills him, [is held to be a fool] here, because he knows nothing, and he is an ignorant man. Here, in Christianity, he who is led by reason alone is called *animal* and is held to be a beast, because, just as one needs to use reason there, among men, so that they won't call you "beast," just so here, so that they won't call you "beast" in the things of the spirit of God: if you aren't led by the wisdom, by the counsel, by the opinion of God, let them call you "animal:" because what is there called "sensuality" is here, among the things of God, called "reason." Behold how many people go about deceived, how few there are who know themselves! What is this? That, although you have as high a judgment as you can, know that you cannot manage to know the wisdom of God through your own knowing; although you reach out as far as you can, you cannot manage to know the spirit of God, you cannot know what fulfills you; although you are an Aristotle, that knowing does no more for you; you cannot, through this [knowing], know the knowing of God, unless you deny your knowing and your reason and you hold yourself back, so that you do not know nor understand anything.

It is more necessary for you to become a fool than to become very lettered; and this is one of the great battles and one of the most difficult to conquer for those who have studied and are accustomed to reasoning and disputing, and for giving proofs through arguments and subtleties: to become the children of whom Jesus Christ speaks, to become those who do not know nor understand anything, who cannot be healed unless God succors them. It is more necessary for one to deny oneself than to become a doctor in theology. I said: Where does it come from, this scuffle about the Most Holy Sacrament, this imagining if the body of Christ is here or not? From your knowing, and from your not wanting to abase your understanding and simply believe in what Jesus Christ says, but rather from your wanting to prove it by your own judgment, and convince yourself that all this could be explained by reason. Then, if you are to follow Jesus Christ, you have to deny that judgment; you have to abandon your scrutinizing of all curiosities, which brings with itself the proving of things through reason. Where do they come from, the anguishes you have, those discontents, that never finding yourself well, that never contenting yourself with a thing that befalls you, since it seems that nothing goes well for you? From your own opinion, from your thinking that there shouldn't be a single thing against you, from it not being as you would like and as would make you content. As is the tree, so is the fruit that is born of it; and never do we see anything born from our own opinion except that; through that, you have anguishes, because you are guided by your opinion and desire. Where does it come from, what you say: "Oh, what I desired has not occurred! I never wanted anything except that it happen as I wanted; the exact opposite befalls me in everything. Then wouldn't this be better, and [wouldn't it be better] for this to happen in this way? God knows best, but I'd much rather He always do whatever I want, and what seems to me like it would be good for me." Cut out that opinion [of yours], for it doesn't know whether it would be good if what you wanted came to pass; for what occurred here is what will fulfill you, though what happened is what you were so concerned about. Beware, for you don't know what is best for yourself. Because of this, don't think later of saying, "I want this; I don't want that." Set the axe to the root of that tree and cut it down; cut away that opinion, and you will rest, then you will have calm; nothing will happen, however contrary it be to what you want, that will give you any pain; take away that root, and you will have joy, you will have peace. As the Apostle says: *Brothers, may the Lord fill you with delight and peace.*[402]

Be Ruled by God's Opinion

"What does living in peace consist in?" In believing that God takes care of what will fulfill you; in your being ruled by His opinion; in believing that that is the best, although it may not seem so to your own judgment. Take away, take away, then, that opinion; rip yourself away from what you know, from what you want, from what seems to you like it would fulfill you. "And if I separate myself from my opinion, in whom will I remain, Father? Whom will I follow?" Draw near to the knowledge of God. Be ruled by the opinion of God alone. Deny yourself and follow Christ. Woe is you, for, when you act according to God's opinion, it weighs on you, and when you do what you want, it pleases you! When you think that the will of God is to be done, you are afraid; and when what your own [will] wants, you rejoice. It should be the opposite. Is it not better for you to trust in God than in yourself? Is it not better to draw near to God than to draw near yourself? Cast all this away. Woe is you, for you don't know what fulfills you. You will never come to Christ if you don't cast away that opinion of yours and if you act like a beast, whose eyes snare it to draw it to drink. *I have become a beast of burden before You.*[403] The prophet David said: "Lord, *what a beast*

402 *Dominus repleat vos omni gaudio et pace.* Rom 15:13.

403 *Ut iumentum factus sum apud te.* Ps 73:22.

am I, for I do not know what fulfills me: What more is a beast than he who knows nothing?"

Ask it of a man: say, "Are you fulfilled by getting married?"

"I don't know; God knows."

"Is being a friar or nun something that fulfills you?"

"I don't know; God knows."

"Does it seem good to you to go out in the morning to handle such or such an affair in the plaza?"

"I don't know."

"Is it good for you to go out on a weekday to buy what you need?"

"I don't know; God knows."

He says "no" to everything. Then what more is a beast than he who knows nothing, and what more is knowing than having God with you? *And I am always with you*, says God.[404] This is the good wisdom of those whom God is with, who are guided by the counsel and opinion of God; and little is the knowledge of those who want to be guided by their own head and opinion. God reproaches this greatly, and He promises to punish it. *I will destroy the counsels of the prudent, and the wisdom of the wise I will reproach.*[405] "Why is it," says God, "that the world is so deceived by the knowledge of those who are wise in their own eyes? Then *I will destroy the counsels of prudent men like them, and I will reproach the wisdom of those wise men.*" Let us deny, brother, our own knowledge, and let us hang onto the knowledge of God. Guide, Lord, and we will follow You; Your counsel is worth more than mine, although it seems tough to me; Your erring, if it were so that You could err, Lord, is worth more than my being right. Take away that opinion, cut off that confidence you have in your own knowledge.

Is there more? What matters this doctrine for nuns and for today's saint? How well did Saint Francis do this! He was so an

---

404 *Et ero semper tecum.* Ps 73:23.

405 *Destruam consilia prudentum et sapientium saptientiam reprobabo.* 1 Cor 1:19.

enemy of following his own opinion or of being ruled by himself that he did not want to follow his own opinion even unto wandering in the street. Going along once, walking, he said to his companion: "Brother, by your life, may you command me on this road, and I will obey you and serve you, and don't do anything else except rule me and tell me what I have to do." Because he knew how great an evil was his own opinion. You will say: "He whose opinion you command me to follow, can he not be deceived?" Yes, but God will give him grace, so that, when he counsels you, he will not err in this. A great good is it to have denied your own will, to be subject, and to have another command you, and for you to obey him! You will know how great a good you have. I said: if someone tells you, "Brother, I have to go through that river and through the midst of that silt. Yet, I have very weak legs; if I walk on my feet, I will fall and I will hurt myself. By your life, may you walk me across on your shoulders, since you have tougher legs than I." Would it seem a great madness for someone to say such a thing to you? But that is what it is to be subject to and to be ruled by another's opinion: to say that he who counsels you and rules you takes the labor on his back. Isn't it better for you to follow another's opinion? How many times has it happened to you that, by looking out a window, you fell into a sin, because you looked out in order to follow your own opinion? How many other times [did you fall] into other sins, by your being ruled by your own head? How many times have you wept so that God would give you what you so desire, and what seems would fulfill you, and would be good for you, and with which you would have rest! Isn't it better that you walk with another's feet and that one other than yourself cross you over?

Certain it is that, if the danger of commanding and the security of obeying is considered, we would flee heaven and earth in order to not command. How I am labored and pained over thinking if I've counseled you well, and how careless and happy is the other one, saying: "That one commanded me; I know no more!" The nun says:

"God does not command me to obey myself, but rather my abbess; by this, I am fulfilled; I don't know anything; she looks to what she commands, for God will demand it of her, if it is not good; I am obliged to do no more than obey." What! Is there such great good in the world? Is it possible? What will you have to say on the day of judgment? My prelate will be asked for an account of what he commanded me, for I know nothing, if I did well or if not. A great thing is it to say: "Pass through heaven, and I will pass over upon your shoulders." Ladies, you have a great good in being subjects, in God's having given you someone who commands you, and whom you should obey, and by whose opinion you should be ruled, instead of by your own. Know how to thank Him; if not, God will chastise you, as He is wont to do to those who fail to recognize the mercies they receive from Him. He who does not know the good he has, what does he deserve? That it be taken from him. What does he deserve, he who does not know how great a good it is to obey? That he be made to command, and be given burdens, and stumble and fall under them, and see the dangers there are in commanding. If you do not know the good there is in not being ruled by your own opinion and by not doing what you want, God will punish you by giving you what seems good to you, and you will think it a mercy, and it will be a punishment.

Deny Your Will Too, and Take Up Your Cross

Moving on. What more do you have to deny? Also your will, your appetites, your desires, your evil inclinations, all this you have to abandon if you are to follow Jesus Christ. Who is there who escapes these faults? Who is there who has not a single remorse? Oh, what that so-and-so did to me! Oh, he didn't speak to me like he usually does! Oh, he didn't take off his cap for me! Oh—I don't know what! A thousand miseries are never lacking. You will take all this away. Nothing will remain; you will be blank, plain as a parchment that is stripped of all its flesh for writing. Take away [that malice,] that evil condition; take away all those evils, if God is to write His wisdom and the gifts of His grace in your soul. It has to be clean, plain, shining; it must have not even a little hair nor a little spot; you have to take away all its flesh. "Lord, so-and-so did me this injury; if, before he did it to me, I loved him well, now I love him more. For love of you, I labor to conquer my fantasy and my pride, to let go of my passions; but I want to pass everything by in order to serve You." To deny yourself, you have to detest yourself; nothing of yourself must remain in you; you have to take away that opinion of yours; you have to deny your appetites, your passions; you have to deny your gluttony, your lust, your ill-will, your pride, your envy. It's clear that, if you are to follow Christ, you have to abandon all this. Oh, what quarrels would be excused at home, ladies, if you denied yourselves! What shortcuts you would take, what calm would your heart have! There would be nothing that is tough for you. Deny your sensuality; deny all the pleasure of this perishing life; deny your own will and opinion, and *take up your cross and follow Jesus Christ.*[406]

"And what is the cross, Father?" The neighbor who persecutes you, hunger, poverty, nakedness, need, to suffer the evil condition of persons with whom you can't avoid dealing, dishonor, infirmities, labors, whatever they be; and all this is nothing: you yourself are a cross to yourself, you yourself persecute yourself. *No one is harmed except by himself.*[407] You alone do wrong to yourself; no one annoys you; no one persecutes you; don't complain about anyone except yourself; you are your own perdition; you yourself are your destruction; don't talk about anyone else. Oh, how tough a thing this is: *I myself do ill to myself!*[408] Do you say that you love yourself

---

406 See Mt 16:24.

407 *Nemo laeditur nisi a se ipso.* This is the Latin title of a treatise by St. John Chrysostom; see PG 52:459–480. There is an English translation by Philip Schaff under the title "No One Can Harm the Man Who Does Not Harm Himself," readily available in the public domain.

408 *Factus sum mihimet ipsi gravis.* Jb 7:20.

well, and do you stab yourself? Each time that you offend God, it's a stab that pierces you with sadness of soul, and do you say that you don't abhor yourself but rather love yourself? "Oh, what evil I do to myself! Oh, if I were alone, then I would be good! Oh, if I didn't converse with so-and-so, then I could serve God well! Oh, if I hadn't passed through that street, I wouldn't have offended God so much! Oh, if I left the company of so-and-so, then I could seclude myself in order to live well! But this is a great nuisance to me." Go to the desert, and enclose yourself, and enclose yourself again, and place yourself between four walls where no one will come to you from any side, where you do not see, do not hear, do not deal with anyone, and you will see that nothing profits you, because what does you ill is with you. What causes you to be lost is within you; you give yourself death with your own hands, and you are contrary and prejudiced against yourself. And thus the patriarch Job complained to God, saying: *Why did You put me against You, Lord*?[409] You are pure, and I, filthy; You, love itself, and I, all quarrels; You, humble, and I, proud; You, merciful, and I, a hardened one.

Why did You put me against You, Lord?

"I?" Says God. "You're a trickster, for you're lying. Adam made you like this; the devil made you as you are, for I created you good, as you seemed to Me: humble, chaste, loving, caring, meek. You yourself are against you, you are the cause of all your labors."

Because you have no love for Christ, because of this, persecutions overwhelm you. Because you have no patience, suffering infirmities and other labors, any whatsoever, goes badly for you. Because you don't want to give a little bit of labor to your flesh, being chaste goes badly for you. Because you want everyone to honor you and be subdued and obedient [to you], being humble goes badly for you. Because you have a bad condition, you don't get along with everyone. Because you act according to your own will and you want everything to be done as you want and to your taste, you wander

---

409 Jb 7:20.

about so discontent that nothing seems good to you. "Then, Lord, what will I do?" Humble yourself, abandon your own opinion, don't will that your own will be done; be content with what befalls you, although it be very adverse, thinking about how everything comes to you from the hand of God. You cannot follow Jesus Christ with rest; you have to labor to wear out body and soul. *Foris pugnae, intus timores*, says the Apostle. *Outside* we pass through *wars, and within* our souls, *fears*.[410]

"All of this, then, you have to do. He who is to follow Me has to suffer himself and others and follow after Me."

"Lord, how much can You ask? Can it cost us so much to go after you? You command us to do so many things that we do nothing. You tell us so much—to abandon our opinions, to not want our wills to be done in regards to anything in the world, to pardon those who injure us, to be chaste, humble, meek—that we don't know what to do, and we do nothing. Who makes me fold my hand?[411] It seems, Lord, that you leave it in my hands whether to follow You. It seems a tough thing for me. I don't know what to choose: to follow You with labors or, in order to not give up my delights, to not follow You. I don't know."

Jesus Christ said this: that *he who wants to follow Him has to take up his cross and deny his will*, and woe to him who doesn't follow Him! What will you do, O sad you?[412]

They Abandoned Me, the Living Font, and Made for Themselves Some Broken Cisterns

Let's enter the story: Who will you follow if you don't follow Christ? Where will you go, O miserable you? Look first at what you do and whom you will follow. Ask, get informed about the road. *Stand*

---

[410] 2 Cor 7:5.

[411] The terminology is that of a card game, more literally, "Who puts me back in the deck?"

[412] See Mt 16:24–26.

along the ways and ask about the ancient paths.[413] Would you rather follow your will than that of God? Ask yourself which is better: following Jesus Christ with labors or the devil with delights; going to heaven by denying your own will or to hell by following your own opinion? *Prepare yourselves in the ancient paths*, says God, *and ask about the road.*

Oh, if we prepared ourselves to ask him who's going along the road, "Brother, which is the better road, that which, by labors, brings one to heaven, or that which, by delights, brings one to hell?" Oh, if you asked the sad one, who has been in hell for so many years, in torments that will not end: "Brother, what did you sow that you reaped so? By what road did you come to such misery, to such hunger, to such torments, from which you will never, as long as God is God, depart? What path brought you to such evil?"

Oh, if you asked him who is in heaven: "Brother, how did you sow, that you reaped so? By what way did you come to such good? What road did you take, so that you found such happiness, such satisfaction, such content, such blessedness, that will never end for you?"

Oh, if you asked, brother! What will you do, you who follow your own will, where nothing that one wills is done, but rather the opposite of what one's will desires? Prepare yourselves in the ancient paths, and ask which is the good road, and walk on it, and *you will find rest for your souls* at the end of the journey, even though, now, it's bland to you. Ask Jesus Christ, who has walked this road and is in heaven: "Lord, what road did You find in this life? By what way did You come to where You are?" By the road of necessities, of labors, which never had a moment of rest while He lived in this life. Take heed; and since you have to go, if you think you'll come to where He is, which road do you want to follow? O sad one! If you don't want to follow Christ, what will you do? If you don't want to pardon him who has injured you, if you don't want to abandon your ugly and filthy delights, what will you do?

---

413 *State super vias, et interrogate de semitis antiquis.* Jer 6:16.

Where will you go? What road is it that you take? Where do you think you'll go at the end of such a life?

"Oh, Father, how very difficult it is for me to conquer my passions and not do what my sensuality asks of me! I love so-and-so a lot; oh, how I can't leave her! How do you want me, Father, to pardon the one who did me such evil?" Oh, unfortunate you! *Spiderwebs you weave*[414] deceiving and perishing is this sad life; you don't have to endure it forever; soon you'll be done with it. O sad one, in what you think holds pleasure, there is sadness; in what you think holds rest, there is labor. *Death in the pot; death in the pot.*[415] In what seems to you like life, there is death; in what seems to you like gain, there is loss; in what seems to you like roses, there are many cruel thorns. *Death in the pot.* Beware, for, although it seems sweet to you, it is bitter; don't drink it, for you'll die. O sad one! May God heal you and enlighten you; may He open your eyes to who He is. Every time I read this, I'm terrified. God says through the prophet Jeremiah: *Be terrified, heavens, of what* I say here; *doors of the heavens, fall open with terror.*[416] It seems that, when a wise man marvels at something and is terrified of it, it moves others to see much in it and to be terrified too. *Be terrified, heavens.* What will they be terrified of, Lord? Of what is done in those streets; of what happens in those plazas, and what we see each day before our eyes, and yet we don't look at it; of what seems to us such trifling things that we take no notice of them; since God commands that *the heavens be terrified* and *their gates fall open with terror* at it.

"What have these men done, Lord?" *They abandoned Me, the font of living water; they dug for themselves shattered cisterns that aren't able to hold waters.*[417] Oh abject Majesty of God. Oh prize despised, so

---

414 Is 59:5.

415 2 Kgs 4:40.

416 Jer 2:12.

417 *Dereliquerunt me, fontem aqaue vivae; foderunt sibi cisternes dissipatas, quae continere non valent aquas.* Jer 2:13.

badly known, joy and sweetness, blessedness considered little! And don't you see how much reason God has for complaining? *They abandoned Me, the font of living water.* Now don't you see which name He was to bear? He says that He is *font of living water*. They abandoned Me, for I had a thousand rests; I am water which kills their thirst; I would refresh the dryness of their souls; I would kill their hunger; I would cover their nakedness; I would remedy their needs; I would give them a rest in place of the labors that they had spent, to give them contentment in place of all the adversity that befell them here; their souls would thirst for a sweetness that would make them forget all the bitterness over there. But *they abandoned Me, font of living water, and they made for themselves shattered cisterns*, destroyed, in which to have water to kill their thirst. *They cannot hold a drop*. They made destroyed, stinking, slimy, filthy cisterns that cannot hold clear water.

What kind of cistern do you drink from? Tell me. What kind is it, oh sad one? And don't you see that there is no water in it to refresh and kill the thirst of your soul, but rather [water] which stinks and doubles your thirst? What's in it, tell me? What's in that sin? What's in that love of your own honor, in that fantasy, in that vainglory? What do you have that holds you so much? What's in the love of that money of yours? What's in the taste of the delight of the flesh? What's in that wanting to follow your own opinion and to always have your will be done? Take off the mask; beware, for evil comes beneath what seems so good to you; in that which brings such peace and security, there is war, and your nosy enemy comes. Don't take it without seeing what kind of thing it is. Say to it: "Reveal yourself, traitor, for you come masked; take off the mask, and let's see who you are and what you bring." First, examine very closely what he brings you and what he carries to you; don't let yourself be deceived, for God's sake. Watch out, for you lose God if you do that sin! Whom do you want to follow—tell me, oh unfortunate you—if you don't follow Christ? What will you do? Where will you go? How will you be able to live without Jesus Christ? In what state will you find yourself without Him, for you will have neither joy nor rest, nor a good hour nor moment?

This is a tough thing. What will we do? Jesus Christ tells us what we have to do. *He who wants to come after Me, let him deny himself and take up his cross and follow Me.*[418] "Who wants to come after Me?" Say: "Lord, it seems necessary to me that I follow You, on any condition, since following You matters so much to us." Then he who is to follow Him, let him deny himself.

Labors, the Beginning of Francis's Good

Now let us look at Saint Francis [of Assisi], let us see what that blessed saint did. He was a young bachelor, a rich merchant who sold fabrics and bargained very well in order to sell them very dear, and he even lied sometimes, as is done today: Who doubts it? God told him: "Deny yourself, Francis; abandon this, and follow Me." There's no one who understands that, Lord. Saint Francis hears nothing of that. He was thinking of how to enrich himself, how to be very honored, and how to get married; and the eyes of God were watching from heaven. "Abandon that; deny yourself, Francis." You won't succeed in this, Lord, unless You use another means.

Now let us the see the method God used to draw him, so that he would follow Him. God inspired him to give him great mercy for the poor; he began to give great alms. He began with mercy, do you see? And he promised that no poor man would come to him and ask him for the love of God to whom he would not give alms, little or great.[419] Will the rivers run and the sea not run? Saint Bernard says, "There is mercy in a little man so that he is pained for and has compassion on the labors of a neighbor, and will there not be some

---

418 Mt 16:24.

419 See St. Bonaventure's *Major Life of St. Francis* I.I.1. Most likely it was Bonaventure's *Life* that St. John was familiar with.

in God for us?"[420] Now, Saint Francis was in his shop, among his fabrics, and God called to him: "Deny yourself, Francis, and follow Me." It didn't work. Don't you understand? "But wait," says God, "I will make you hear." He gives him a very great infirmity, and after that, a fear of dying and of going to hell. Don't speak ill of infirmities or of labors. See how God sends them for our good. Saint Francis had a most great fear. *The sinners were struck* with fear *in Sion.*[421] He begins to tremble like King Baltazar and like Nebuchadnezzar, for it is recounted of him that he put one foot on the other with fear when God dragged them into infirmities. The good Francis was of a little size; he begins to tremble and God [begins] to put fear into him, like the mother who takes the child and puts him at the mouth of the well and acts as if she intends to lower him down because of some little thing that the boy has done, and he begins to tremble and say: "Oh my mother, I won't do it anymore; don't throw me in!" God gives him infirmity; He lashes Saint Francis; God teaches him the brevity of this deceitful life; he begins to think, "Ah, I'm going to die tomorrow, I won't come back here anymore, I don't know where I'm going to go; all my life I've lived so badly, in such forgetfulness of God; how many times has God called me, pleading me to follow Him, *and* I didn't want to answer Him; there is hell for the evil, where they who lived as I have are punished; oh sad me, what will I do, for, perhaps, God won't want to listen me, since I never wanted to listen to Him! Oh Lord, no more, by who You are; if You did this to amend me, I will do it." "Yes indeed, Francis; that is what I wanted." Do you see that infirmity and terror did what benefits, kind treatment could not; what sermons, confessors, admonitions, inspirations from God could not do?

---

420 Compare St. Bernard, *On the Manner of Living Well*, Ch. XIV–XV: "Certainly, he does not love his neighbor who does not succor him in need. The more we succor our neighbors in need through compassion, that much more will we draw near the Creator . . . He who has mercy on another will gain mercy from God" (PL 184:1225A, 1226A).

421 *Conterriti sunt peccatores in Sion.* Is 33:14.

The Cross Remains Impressed on the Melted Soul of the Saint

He was good, and God showed him, one night—I don't know if it was in prayer or in dreams—a very rich, very bright room, all of gold, and all around, full of blazons[422] of crosses; and He told him: "All of this I will give you, Francis, and much more, if you are a man fit for carrying those banners you see and for being a very good captain of My Cross." Meaning, if he would consider it an honor to take on labors with much strength and much willingness, if he would prize himself on being dishonored and run off and beat down by everyone, if he would suffer much hunger, much nakedness, many needs, and [suffer it] that everyone run him off and consider him a madman, if he would be saddened and made disconsolate by something that went against him. This, then, God intended to say to him in asking him if he would carry the banner of the Cross. Saint Francis departed from there so frightened, so out of himself, so changed from what he was before; everything seemed upside-down to him. All that he took rest in before was bland to him; what delighted him before now gave him profound sadness. He used to have such a great worry about the things of this life that he couldn't bear them. He went away so consoled! He had taken so great a delight! And, since it had happened so quickly, he didn't know what had befallen him. As the patriarch Job said of this: *In his hands he hides the light, and he orders it to come again, so that he would announce it to his friend, that it is his possession, so that he can ascend to it.*[423] He went away saying: "Lord, what is this? Oh, how great a sweetness, oh what a flavor! If it lasted long, what would it

---

422 *Escudo* can mean "shield" in general, but it can also refer to a coat of arms, or blazon, which seems the intended meaning here. For an account of this vision, see St. Bonaventure's *Major Life of St. Francis* I.I.3.

423 *In manibus abscondit lucem, et praecepit ei ut rursus adveniat ad nuntiandum de ea amico suo; quae possessio ei sit, ut ad eam possit ascendere.* Jb 36:32–33.

be? If You give such a thing to Your friends during this life full of labors, what is it that You have prepared for them over there?" Very quickly this delight passed away, because this is God's condition: *He hides the light between His hands, and He commands it to come appear again, and He gives His friends to understand that it is His possession and how he can ascend to Him.*

God does this with His friends. At the beginning, He lets them understand a little bit, so that they won't think they're laboring in vain and going after an uncertain thing; He gives them a little bit of a taste of Himself; He delights them, regales them, shows Himself to them, opens their eyes, and makes the light appear, so that they might see how sweet a thing He is. He tells them: "Taste Me here, I am your possession; I am all of the good that you have; your rest, your satisfaction, your blessedness; see Me here; well can you come to Me." And when they don't look at these things, He makes them disappear. Before, they thought that that flavor was to endure; now, they have nothing; so He takes Himself away from them and makes that flavor disappear, and labor comes. He who has experienced this from Him then loses the taste of the things of this life; and he who has not lost it, even though he well knows what is here, was not given to taste what is over there.

Later Saint Francis said: "Lord, how do You want me to serve You? In what state? As monk or married? Give me Your grace, so that I might choose the right state in which to please You." He called so much, he cried so much, he persevered so much in this, that God heard him, and Jesus Christ crucified appeared to him and spoke to him from the Cross, and told him: "Francis, *if you want to come after Me, deny yourself and take up your cross and follow Me.*"[424] Said and done. He arose from there, and it wasn't necessary to tell him a second time. That is the gift of the elect and the predestined of God, that they would say and then do, because God gives them the grace so to fulfill it. God tells them, "Do this," and He then gives them the

---

[424] Mt 16:24.

grace to put it in action, although they do it freely. Jesus Christ told him, then, "Abandon that, Francis, and follow Me." The story says that his soul was melted.[425] *Melted*, moved, *is my heart* by the words of my Lord.[426] Just so, if you press a seal on hard wax, it does not seal or leave a mark; but when the wax is melted and soft, the seal impresses on it much better. So that is the sign that you are of the elect: if you melt when God calls you, if you become very soft at the call of God. It profits nothing to feel that God is calling you if there's nothing more than this, and your soul still remains hard. The call that is not that of the elect makes you feel your misery, but yet you remain in it; but if you melt at God's speech, if you say, "Oh sad me, what will be done with me? What shall I do? What am I wasting my life with? What a deceit this is, to have my rest here, in so perishing a thing? I want to abandon so deceitful a thing; tomorrow I will die, I will leave everything here," this is the call of friends. *A thing of fire is Your word, Lord.*[427] Your call burns everything, melts everything.

The Cross remained so impressed upon Saint Francis's bowels; his heart remained so melted, so soft, that it's frightening. But how well [these words] were fulfilled in him: "*Set Me as a seal on your heart, love Me*, remember Me, impress Me on your bowels; transform yourself into Me through love; and *place Me too as a seal on your arm*, through works, *because love is as strong as death.*"[428] Jesus Christ kept him so sealed that, if he went on the road and saw some little lamb

---

425 St. Bonaventure's *Major Life of St. Francis* I.I.5 (in Benen Fahy's translation) uses this exact word: "Then Jesus Christ appeared to him, hanging on his cross. His soul melted at the sight and the memory of Christ's passion was impressed on the depths of his heart." See *St. Francis of Assisi: Writings and Early Biographies: English Omnibus of the Sources for the Life of St. Francis,* ed. Marion A. Habig (Quincy, IL: Franciscan Press, 1991), I:639.

426 *Anima mea liquefacta est.* Sg 5:6.

427 *Ignitum eloquium tuum, Domine, vehementer.* Ps 119:140.

428 *Pone me ut signaculum super cor tuum, et ut signaculum super brachium tuum; quia fortis est ut mors dilectio.* Sg 8:6.

that couldn't walk, he took it on his shoulders and cried with it and carried it to its mother.

"What is this, Francis? Why are you crying?"

"I'm remembering Our Lord Jesus Christ, how, being so innocent, He was so mistreated; being so just and so meek, they did such cruelties to Him."

When he heard some [hammer] blows, then he remembered the blows of the hammer with which they nailed Jesus Christ to the Cross. How he carried Jesus Christ, sealed, in everything he said, saw, and heard!

He was very badly struck by all infirmities; he was constipated; he vomited blood all night; he had abdominal pain, gout; he was hydropic[429] and blind from weeping for his sins. He was very sick, for, moved by compassion, a friar, his companion, told him: "Brother, pray now to God that He would reduce the time of His wrath towards you a little bit and heal you. See how great a shame it is to see you as you are."

Saint Francis took great pain from this: "Go away, for the love of God; don't look at what you've said. If I hadn't known you and conversed with you all my life, I would separate myself from you; I would never more deal with a man who spoke to me so. What! Don't I know the mercies God sent me? You call this the wrath of God?" he said.[430]

"Mercy, and great. I will never know goods and gifts as great as these infirmities! Don't speak so, for the love of God." And, having said this, he threw himself off of his low bed and began to give himself blows.

"Where does this come from?" From thinking of the Crucified. There this doctrine was taught to him. For he carried nothing else

---

429 That is, he was afflicted with dropsy, or edema; in the past, the term was more focused on the symptom of insatiable thirst than on the primary symptom (swelling of the body with fluid, often due to congestive heart failure).

430 See *Saint Francis of Assisi: Omnibus of Sources*, I:738.

before his eyes except Jesus Christ placed on the Cross, as He first appeared to him! You who are accustomed to thinking of Christ's Passion, look at where Jesus Christ called you, and think more on that step; if the crucifixion appears to you, I mean to say, if the crucified Christ comes to your thought more often, give yourself to thinking much of Him; if when He carried the Cross on His back, if when He was at the column, finally, that which comes to your thought more often, think more on that, because it is a sign that God wants you to follow Him through it.

I Don't Want Any Other Father but You, Lord

Saint Francis, then, went to a cave. He was a great friend of being alone and in a dark place. Francis went to solitude. *I will bring my beloved to solitude, and I will give her milk there, and I will speak to her heart.*[431] He was, then, there in that cave, he wept there, he groaned for his sins. "Oh light that illumined the blindness of my soul! And what has become of me? How have I offended You? How have I not loved You? How did I find myself living without You? What do You want me to do, Lord?" He was in doubt: "Should I depart from here or should I stay here, doing penance?" God told him: "Walk on, coward, depart from here."[432] He departed and dressed in a cloak of sackcloth, and he girded himself with a rope, and thus he walked through the streets. Going forth, boys and men who knew as little as [the boys] began to say after him: "Gone crazy, gone crazy!" Since they had seen him before, dressed in silk, on horseback, with serving-boys, with triumphs, everyone said: "Gone crazy!" And the boys went over to pull back his cloak and smear mud on his face.

---

431 *Ego deducam dilectam meam in solitudinem, et lactabo eam et loquar ad cor eius.* Hos 2:14.

432 In St. Bonaventure's *Major Life of St. Francis* I.II.2, it is Francis who rebukes himself as a coward during his seclusion in a cave, not God. Afterwards, he wanders through the streets shouting curses and rebukes at himself, which is what prompted his father to lock him up.

The servant of God suffered this with great patience, and he blessed God. Then they all turned against him, and his father shouted out: "Oh, how this traitor dishonors me!"

You see the war here. Oh spiritual son, and [the son] of a crazy father and mother! The father takes him and throws him out, seeing his withdrawn son, who, if he used to stroll about and dress up, does it no longer; if he used to go about committing a thousand scoundrelisms, now he has abandoned them. When the daughter is a window-gazer or a gossip, then the parents are very happy; when she secludes herself, when they see that she doesn't want to marry, that she communes, that she confesses often, then [they cry out], "Oh, how wicked a woman she is! Oh, how she dishonors us! Chains!" *And they wanted to lay hold of him, saying to themselves, "For he's become mad."*[433] (Saint Mark, about Christ the Lord).[434] Do you understand well what the world wants? To tie up wisdom, prudence, tact, harmony with God, saying that it's gone crazy.

His father, then, takes Saint Francis and ties him up, lashes him.[435] "Oh, this madman who dishonors me!" The mother, being more tender, and because she had compassion upon seeing him treated this way, released him; and Saint Francis said to his father: "Lord, if you have been so dishonored by what your son is, let's go before the provisor,[436] and I will say there that I am not your son, and I will renounce all right to be your son." They went and got a scribe, and then he said: "Sir, until now, I bore the title of my father's son; I say now that I am not his son, nor do I consider myself such, now and as long as I live." Having said this, he stripped himself there, before all, and he remained in live leather,[437]

---

433 *Et voluerunt tenere eum sui dicentes: quoniam in furorem versus est.* Mk 3:21.

434 *De Cristo Domino.*

435 For the story of Francis's imprisonment by his father, freeing by his mother, and rejection of his family in the presence of the bishop (not a provisor, as St. John has it), see St. Bonaventure's *Major Life of St. Francis* I.II.2–4.

436 A diocesan judge in charge of churchly affairs, appointed by the bishop.

437 A Spanish idiom meaning "completely naked."

as his mother bore him, without father, without mother, without estate, without the favor of relatives nor of friends. He renounced all of it, none of it remained for him. Oh, how well he fulfilled the Gospel to the letter: how could there be any more that needs to be done! How well it comes now: *My father and my mother have abandoned me, and the Lord took me under His protection*![438] "*Our Father, Who art in heaven, hallowed be Your Name*. I don't want any other father but You, Lord; if You bore the Cross, I want a Cross; if You were poor, for You had no place where to lay Your head[439]—such was Your extreme need—I want to be poor; if You suffered much thirst, much hunger, much cold, much nakedness, I, too, want it so." His father cursed him, and he went to a farmer and said to him: "Brother, my father curses me; in place of his curses, do you bless me." The good man tossed him a blessing and said to him: "May you be blessed by God, for so blessed and so fortunate has He made you!"

Little Flowers of Saint Francis[440]

He walked away from there, so humble, so low, so knocked down and despised by all. They made no more fuss about him than about a bit of silt. He was so little in his own esteem that, if an evil thought came to him, he then shouted out, saying, "Oh, how you consider me good, and I am a hypocrite!" And he brought himself, while lashing himself, to the pillory; and there he told the evil he had done, so that all would hear.[441] This isn't done now: rather, we lock

438 *Pater meus et mater mea dereliquerunt me, Dominus autem assumpsit me.* Ps 27:10.

439 Mt 6:9; Lk 11:2.

440 Despite this title, the following stories are not found in the *Fioretti*—which mainly focuses on stories involving St. Francis's companions—but rather in other lives and legends of St. Francis.

441 This recalls St. Francis's public self-rebuke for being a "glutton," as recounted in St. Bonaventure's *Major Life of St. Francis* I.VI.2.

up the faults we have with seven keys, and we want no one to know them. How humble, how little, how simple was this blessed saint!

If he went through that field and called to the birds, they came and blessed him. Behold: if we always endured in the innocence of Adam, before he sinned, all creatures would obey us. So those who now, through the grace of God, attain to that innocence, all things obey them, just like back then. If he commanded the birds to sing, they did it; and he called to them when he said Matins, and he said one verse, and they another; and he had different birds to sing, some at one hour, and others at another. He very much loved those little birds that they call crested larks, because he said that they looked like friars [due to] those crests of feathers they have upon their heads.[442]

He once had a sickness of the eyes, and they wanted to cauterize them with fire, and as he saw the iron already heated, made white by the embers, and they wanted to put it on his eye, he was afraid, and he said to it, "Brother Fire, I command you, in the name of Our Lord Jesus Christ, do not burn me," and the fire obeyed him; he felt not a thing. He called all things "brothers:" little lambs, birds, everything.[443]

He was a great friend of music, and there was a friar in the monastery who played the vihuela[444] very well, and he once begged him, "Brother, for the love of God, since I have a great desire to hear you play, may you give me a little bit of music."

The friar answered him, "Jesus, Father, don't order me to do such a thing, to return now to what I have abandoned for so many years

442 For the sermons to the birds, see St. Bonaventure's *Major Life of St. Francis* I.XII.3–5. St. Francis's love for the crested lark is recounted in the *Legend of Perugia* §110 and the *Mirror of Perfection* §113.

443 For the story of the cauterized eyes, see St. Bonaventure's *Major Life of St. Francis* I.V.9.

444 A fifteenth-century Spanish instrument that is shaped like a guitar but tuned like a lute; the original versions of this story describe the instrument as a lyre.

for love of Jesus Christ. I renounced all that when I entered here; don't order me to do it, Father."

Sir Saint Francis said to him, "Do it now, brother, for it is no offense to God; never is God offended by such trifling things, rather, it is for us to delight in His glory." He never wanted do it for any other [reason] than the one he had said. That night, Sir Saint Francis being in his cell, there came a great thundering of vihuela music, of minstrel songs, of however many genres of music there are, through the street; and all the night the angels, who came with great music, did nothing but wander up and down the street until it was day. "Father, last night, you didn't want to do what I begged of you, so my Lord Jesus Christ sent me this night to console you with very sweet music."[445]

He wandered about preaching, and there was a man who begged him to preach one day, and him later, at the time of the Gospel. He never ever wanted to be ordained for Mass because he said that he was not worthy of taking such an office as that of cleric and that if he met a priest in the street and a canonized saint who was not a priest, that he would do more honor to the priest; he said that, at Mass, all should tremble with reverence for the Son of God, who was there on the altar. Going, then, to preach, at the plea of that man, the good man's serving girl came and said: "What! Don't I get to hear this holy man?" She quickly did her household tasks, and left a boy at the house, and nearly a cauldron of water, very large, placed at the hearth. The girl left the boy alone and closed the door of the house and went to the sermon; while she heard the sermon, the boy fell into the cauldron and was cooked there, and there remained naught but the clean bones alone. The girl arrived before her masters, and when she found the boy dead, she began to weep

---

445 See St. Bonaventure's *Major Life of St. Francis* I.V.11, though St. John's retelling, especially the discussions with the friar, is more reminiscent of the *Legend of Perugia* §24 or Thomas of Celano's *Second Life of St. Francis* II.LXXXIX.126.

and to do great things. They had begged Saint Francis to eat with them, and he did so. And she took the bones and placed them in a chest, and the masters coming, she told them what had happened. You already see what they felt. They said: "It's already done; we'll not now give bad food to this servant of God; later, we'll weep for our sorrow."

They sat down to eat. See how the food tasted to those sad parents! In finishing the meal, Saint Francis said, "I would like some good apples."

The honored guests said, "Certainly, Father, there are none in our house, nor will they be found, since it's not time for them now."

He said again, "Look for some apples for me now, for I have a great desire for them."

The good folk, looking despondently at each other, since they couldn't fulfill that holy man's desire, said to him, "Certainly, Sir, we don't know where they are now."

Then Saint Francis said: "In that chest." And he signaled where the dead boy was.

See what's news for the father! "I certainly don't know if there are apples there."

Saint Francis said: "Go, for there surely are."

The father went and opened the chest and found his son, alive and healthy, seated in the chest with two apples in his two hands. The boy said to the father: "Take, father." And the father took them with great joy and gave them to Saint Francis, and the holy man said: "These are the apples I desired." All blessed God for the great miracle that had been done through the plea of His servant Francis.[446]

There is no count of how many miracles he did. How well God repaid him for the denial of his own will, for taking up his Cross! How's it going for you, Francis? Is this better than selling fabric?

---

446 I've not yet found any source for this horrific story. The closest story I've found is one told of St. Vincent Ferrer (1350–1419), who revived a boy who had been chopped up and cooked by his crazed mother.

What are you more content with: The riches you abandoned, or the labors you found by abandoning them?

He was, one day, trembling with cold, and a brother of his said to him, "Sell me a bit of sweat, Francis, brother."

He answered him, "Certainly; if I don't give it to you, I would have to give it to my Lord Jesus Christ."[447] He said that goodness, being a good man, was not in having many delights, in being very consoled, very visited, very regaled by God, but rather in passing through many labors.

On the road, very tired and dead of hunger, he said to his companion, "There is no pleasure, there is no pleasure fulfilled in this life, Father."

The other said, "How, Father?"

"If we were now at the monastery, and they gave us straw mats and food, that would be good; but they would have to give us a thousand gifts for us to rest from this little labor."

Impression of the Wounds. Death.

He went to Mount La Verna,[448] and standing there one night in prayer, he heard a sound like an arrow[449] and it struck his hand;

---

447 See the *Legend of the Three Companions* §23 and Thomas of Celano's *Second Life of St. Francis* I.VII.12.

448 The Spanish reads *monte Armenio* ("Armenian Mountain"), most likely an error for *monte Alvernia* ("Mount La Verna"). "The Armenian Mountain" is a name for Mount Ararat, where Noah's Ark landed.

449 Saint Francis did not hear this arrow-sound when he received the stigmata; instead, this sound is from the story of Roger of Apulia, a priest who doubted Francis's stigmata. "As the wound of doubt pierced his heart . . . he suddenly felt a heavy blow on his left hand beneath his glove. At the same time he heard a noise like the sound of a javelin being thrown from a catapult" (Bonaventure, *Major Life*, Part II, I.6, in *St. Francis of Assisi: Writings and Early Biographies*, I:752). Roger received painful temporary stigmata, which were removed when he professed his faith in Francis's stigmata and prayed for Francis's intercession. Rather than a "javelin being thrown from a catapult"

and he felt a very great pain from it, and blood began to run from it; and then another arrow came and struck him in the other hand; and then in his two feet and in his side. Fear, fear this. If he were not so humble, God would not have communicated such secrets to him. He greatly concealed the wounds. It did not pass through his thought to have vainglory about these things; but he walked about, hiding them from everyone. He always had his hands covered; no one ever saw the wound in his side, except one of his companions, and he revealed it to him later.[450] He traveled about on a little donkey because he could not walk, due to the wounds on his feet. Two years [after] he died, his order [instituted] and erected its monastery there, on that mountain.[451] One can't say how much there is.[452]

God revealed to him when he was to die, and he told it to his friars; and they sent out a call to a Roman woman, a very holy woman, who had cured him another time, so that she could see him before he died. And God revealed to her, too, when he was to die, and she came then, and he said to the friars: "Go on, don't call her, for she'll come." And then she came.[453] He died on Saturday in the

---

(perhaps a ballista is intended), Jacobus de Voragine's *Golden Legend* describes the sound as "like a bolt shot from a crossbow," which is closer to St. John's telling. See Jacobus de Voragine, *The Golden Legend: Selections*, ed. and tr. Christopher Stace (New York: Penguin Books, 1998), 262.

450 See St. Bonaventure's *Major Life of St. Francis* I.XIII.1–4.

451 Saint Francis was declared a saint in 1228, two years after he died, and the cornerstone for his basilica in Assisi was laid the next day; a church wasn't built on La Verna until 1260. The editor of the Spanish text thinks the missing word here is "before" not "after"; in that case, the sentence would read "Two years before he died, he instituted his order and erected his monastery there, on that mountain." However, the Franciscan Order had been instituted in 1209, whereas the stigmata were received in 1224, and St. Francis died in 1226.

452 Most likely, St. John means, "One cannot tell all the stories there are about St. Francis."

453 Blessed Jacoba (or Giacoma) of Settesoli (1190–1273) was a friend and supporter of St. Francis, so close to him that she was nicknamed "Brother Jacoba." The account of her last visit to Francis—including the gift of her

afternoon. Seeing that his hour had come, he commanded them to bring twelve slices of bread and another for him, and they ate them there in memory of the supper of the Lord Jesus Christ, and he gave them a sermon, greatly recommending humility to them. Then the hour of his death came, and he commanded that they read that gospel: *Before the day of the feast of Passover*, etc.[454] It's very pretty for that hour. See that you don't forget to have them read this to you at the hour of your death. When he was to die, he cast himself on the ground, in order to appear like Jesus Christ, and he begged that they not bury him then, but rather that they wait a little after his death, as with Jesus Christ. There was also, at that time, a friar at the point of death, and when Saint Francis expired, he saw so many angels who carried his soul away with so much joy, and he saw it so resplendent, and he said to him, "Father, plead to our Lord that He might carry me with you." Then the friar died, while saying how he saw Saint Francis, and he also went to heaven. Thus Saint Francis died.[455] There is testimony about all this. We know that, in payment for his labors, for his necessities, for his denying his own opinion and will, God gave him grace here and glory there.

---

famous almond cookies, or *mostaccioli*—is found in the *Legend of Perugia* §101 and the *Mirror of Perfection* §112.

[454] *Ante diem festum Paschae*, etc. Jn 13:1ff.

[455] The general account of St. Francis's last hours and death is found in St. Bonaventure's *Major Life of St. Francis* I.XIV. The eating of bread, in memory of the Last Supper, is found in the *Legend of Perugia* §117 and the *Mirror of Perfection* §88, though the number of brothers present is not specified.

Sermon 80

Awaken Our Sleep, Lord; Arouse Our Care

(November 25: St. Catherine of Alexandria, Sir 2:1–8, 12; Mt 25:1–13)
Given in a monastery of monks

"Vigilate itaque."
"Stay awake, therefore."[456]

Exordium

THOSE who sleep much and have need of getting up very early have need of commending themselves to someone who is awake, who will remember them. It's usual to say: "I slept a lot. I need to wake up; call me." Our Lord Jesus Christ calls us and commands that we keep vigil.[457] He commands us to wake up. It's very important for us to wake up; it does us much profit to keep vigil. We all sleep, and we are all sleepy; we have need of commending ourselves to someone who is staying awake. The Virgin is she who always kept vigil; from the moment she was conceived, she

[456] Mt 25:13.

[457] *Velar* can mean simply "to stay awake," but it can also mean "to keep watch," "to keep vigil," and "to be vigilant." Throughout this sermon, I have tried to pick out the best translation for each use, but the reader should keep these many overlapping meanings in mind while reading.

was always keeping vigil, and because of we who are asleep, God thinks it good to give us some little thing with which we might stay awake, commending us to the Virgin, and let us supplicate her with the angelic salutation, saying, *Ave, Maria.*

Parable of the Virgins: Five Were Prudent and Five Crazy

Stay awake, therefore.[458] The words are taken from the Gospel of Saint Matthew, chapter 25. In our tongue, they say: *Keep watch.* Whatever it be, whatever happens, keep watch. *While all things were in the midst of silence, and it was night.*[459] *At midnight,* in the deepest of sleep, *from the royal seats,* the Wise Man says, *the almighty Word of God came.*[460] At midnight, when we sleep, when sleep has its greatest strength, in the deepest of darkness, God sent His Word. What is this trying to say? *A great doctor descended from heaven, for there was a great sickness on earth.*[461] A great mercy descended, because there was a great misery on the ground. He means to say that, when the Lord came to the world, He found men in midnight, in the deepest of sleep, and so the Lord, our watcher,[462] thus wandered through mountains and valleys and cities, crying out: "Stay awake, stay awake, why are you sleeping?" How much it seems like you should stay awake, and you are sleeping! Haven't you seen some men who arise at midnight asleep, and go out of the house, and wander about, still

---

458 *Vigilate itaque.*

459 *Dum medium silentium tenerent omnia, et nox esset.*

460 This is from the Introit of the Sunday within the Octave of Christmas, also used for the Vigil of Epiphany; the prayer is based on Wisdom 18:14–15.

461 *Descendit de caelo magnus medicus, quia erat in terra magnus infirmus.* See St. Augustine, *Sermon* 175.1: "Take away the sickness, take away the wound, and there is no reason for healing. If a great doctor came from heaven, [it is because] a great sickness lay over the whole globe of the world. For the whole human race was sick" (PL 38:945).

462 *Velador* is related to *velar,* the key verb discussed above. Thus, it can mean "watchman," "one who keeps vigil," "one who stays awake," etc.

sleeping, and it seems to them that they are awake? So it happens: to the men, it seems like they're awake, and they're asleep. Beware, lest you sleep! Christ our Redeemer awakens us not only with words, but with deeds. There is nothing that frightens me so much as to think of the care He had for the work of our salvation, which He carried in His hands, which the Father had commended to Him. What an example for preachers, that we should wander about preaching! And all you preachers and confessors, take profit from this; Our Lord kept so great a vigil that everything we do is nothing in comparison with Him. How You walked with water through streets, through labors; and if there was something men owed, You paid it Yourself! Lord, how You paid for us, for our sins, on the Cross!

This was the office of our Redeemer, to cry out to men: "Stay awake." And, so that this word will remain firm in our memory, He wanted to tell it to us through a parable;[463] because what is said in low and workmanlike comparisons now is what remains firmer in our memory later. Because of this, our God clothed Himself in our humanity. The Word enclosed in a low thing. Do you know that He, the incarnate Word, is a very great thing enclosed in a very little thing? Just so, He wanted His powerful word to be preached in parables and low comparisons; and just so this word, through which He so much wanted to recommend us to stay awake, He preached to us in a parable, and so He tells us in the Gospel: *The kingdom of the heavens is like ten virgins.*[464] "What is the kingdom of the heavens?" It is glory; Christianity is called "the kingdom of the heavens." And, so that we will be like those who are in heaven, we have to do the will of God like them, and we have to live like them, and we have to be like them in our ways of living. *The kingdom of the heavens*—Christianity—*is like ten virgins*, five of whom were prudent, and five were crazy; and it seems they were waiting for a day when they were to go to certain betrothals, to go to receive a bridegroom. They were

463 Literally, a "likeness," "resemblance," or "simile" (*semejanza*).

464 Mt 25:1.

those who were betrothed to Him. "Who are they?" Christianity, to whom the Bridegroom said: "See that you are prepared to enter with Me into the wedding feast, for I will come." "What is the preparation they have to make?" It seems that the bridegroom was a friend of light; He wants them to prepare for it with light. Behold, here is the preparation. The five made provision for it, *they took oil in their oil-jars*; the other five did not take care to take some. At midnight, when sleep was most profound, a great voice resounds, which ought to be a trumpet. All wake up. "What is it?" A powerful voice of strength. The *prudent* ones come, very prim, very composed, with their lamps lit, very stocked with oil. The *fools* come, those who didn't know how to recognize their own madness until prudence was needed, and they found themselves mocked.

What you did not reach in your youth, how will you find it in sickness? *The sluggard said*, etc.[465] *He doesn't want to work because of the cold; he will go begging in the summer.*[466] May God let us understand this. Brother, how are our days spent? What do we waste our time with? Going to the plaza? Returning [home] to eat? Back to the plaza, and back to supper? Beware, for this time is given us in order to reach Him; beware, for, if we do not reach Him here, if, in this life, which is given us in order to gain [Him], we do not reach [Him], we will go begging in the other. If we do not take oil here, in the other life, we will have no light. The Bridegroom is a friend of light, and how will we be found if He finds us in the dark? Let us not see ourselves in such labor, Lord, for the sake of Your goodness and for the sake of who You are. Let not such great harm come to us; let not such a great trick be played on us, so that we find ourselves unstocked, and find ourselves without light, and lose the chance to enter with the Bridegroom. He who does not stock up will go begging, and he won't find someone to give him oil. "Go walk, for what we have is set aside; there's no reason why we should remain

465 *Piger dixit.*

466 Prv 20:4.

without it in order to give some to you. Go walk, go look." Let our ears not hear such a word, by Your mercy. Unfortunate is that soul whose ears will hear such a thing! Is there no reason to keep awake, is there no reason to be always stocked up? "Go walk, we don't have enough for our lamps and yours."

Here, preachers will learn what they teach others; they have to give and leave some for themselves; they have to have enough for themselves and for others; if not, it would be better for them to say, "I only have enough for myself. *Small is the cape; it can't cover two. Narrow is the seat; there's not room for both.*"[467] Why such a sermon, such a confessor, such a counselor, and the man goes away so dry, so cold, and the preacher remains more so, because, having so little oil, we want to give it to another? It profits neither the one nor the other. It's not for all to understand, it's not for all to be kindled; one must have enough to give and to have some left over. It would be better to say: "*So that I won't be lacking, go and look for someone who will give it to you, go to him who sells it.*"[468] Why don't we do this? I, at least, confess my fault here.

May God let that man understand the great mercy that He did him in putting him under another's will, in letting him be ruled by another, so that he doesn't do his own will. It is a most great mercy of God's that one goes through this waist-deep mud, and another goes on his shoulders and doesn't get muddy. It is a great mercy that God does this. Let him who commands look to how he commands; let him who rules look to how he rules; but the one commanded is secure, he doesn't have to look. It's possible that he who commands might sin and offend God, but he who is commanded and obeys serves God most greatly. A great mercy is it that God does for him. In order to please Our Lord, there is no book, there is no revelation, there is nothing so secure as denying one's own will and being ruled by that of another. The Desert Fathers used to say what we laugh at

---

467 *Pallium breve est, utrumque operire non potest.* Is 28:20.

468 Mt 25:9.

now: that obedience is nothing unless it is something beyond [our] nature and against our inclination. A monk had a son, and the prior told him: "Light that oven." He lit it. "Toss your son inside." He tossed him in, and he didn't burn.[469] He said to another, "Go through that river," which had swelled; the river became hard as that ground, and he passed over. "Take that dry straw and water it until it bears fruit."[470] They said: "When they command us only what our reason tells us, there's no worth in that; we do it by our own will." Faith has to be in things that my reason doesn't reach, that I don't reach: that is what I obey. For what I reach and what conforms to my will, I do it, but it's not obedience.

---

469 In the Latin collection of the *Lives of the Fathers (Vitae Patrum)*, this story is found at V.XIV.18 (PL 73:952A–C). In that version, a monk who had three sons who were not in the monastery desired to have them join him; the abbot agreed, and the monk, finding that two of his sons had died, brought the other to live in the monastery. When they arrived, they went to the abbot. "And holding the child whom he had brought forth, he embraced him. And he said to his father, 'Do you love him?' And he said, 'Of course.' Again he said to him, 'Do you really love him?' And he responded, 'Of course.' Hearing this, the abbot then said to him, 'Take him, then, if you love him, and throw him into the furnace, as soon as the furnace is burning.' And the father, taking his son, threw him into the burning furnace. But immediately the furnace became like dew; from this, he acquired glory at that time, like Abraham the patriarch."

470 This story is found in *Lives of the Fathers* IV.26, which tells of a monk named John, renowned for his humility and obedience. "Wanting to more clearly explore whether this virtue of his descended from true faith and profound simplicity of heart, the elder frequently enjoined upon him many things, even superfluous and impossible things," one of which was to plant a stripped stick and water it twice a day; "for the whole space of a year, no infirmity of the body, no occupation with any intervening necessity could hinder him from observing this precept." At the end of the year, his elder "saw how he had kept his command like a divine imperative, with the affection of a simple heart; then, taking pity on his perseverance in so long a labor, approaching the dry stick, he said, 'O son John, did this tree send out roots, or not?' When he said he didn't know, the elder, as if testing if it were now held by its roots, ripped out the stick before him, and, throwing it far away, he ordered his disciple to henceforth cease watering it" (PL 73:831C–832A).

Let us turn to our proposition: "Walk on, for we cannot give to you." On that fearful day of judgment, each one will have so much to do, including understanding how he will give account of himself, that he won't be able to help anyone. No one will be able to avail himself of another. "Walk on, so that you won't be lacking, O unfortunate one!" At the time when you have to eat, are you going to sow? Gentle thing, gentle madness! At the time when you have to dress, do you remember to make the cloak? Now that you have to go out with your light, are you going to look for oil? *The bridegroom comes*, receives the prudent, has taken them with him into his chamber, as at the wedding feast, *closes himself in* with them. *The crazy ones come*. Oh crazy ones, and if you knew what is happening! The door is closed. *Lord, Lord! Bona est vox*: "Good is the sentence," says Saint Jerome.[471] "*Lord, Lord!*" "Who's there?" Five virgins betrothed to You with words of the future. The bridegroom says: "Walk on from here, crazies, for, however much you tell me who you are, your name and office, and claim to me that you are virgins, I do not know you; and, if you want, I will swear it: *Truly, I do not know who you are*." Lord, by Your goodness, let not our ears hear this sentence: *I don't know you*! "You don't speak My language, that isn't My mold, you haven't lived as My brides, we are not as one, you are not to enter with Me into My wedding feast."

We Have to Live in Order to Keep Watch

Lord, what are You trying to say? He concludes, and in this manner, we understand what He wanted to tell us in the parable: "Then go on in this way: be careful about what matters to you. See that you do not sleep; do not be careless in something that matters so much

---

[471] See St. Jerome, *Commentary on the Gospel of Matthew* IV, on Mt 25: "Indeed, an excellent confession it is to call upon the Lord's Name, and the same thing repeated is an indication of faith. But what does it profit you to cry out with your voice what you deny by your works?" (PL 26:185D–186A).

to you." It matters so much to us, for it is commanded us that we do not focus on anything else, that we abandon the other and focus on this alone. Someone says to his steward: "See that you do not let this affair fall from your hand and beware lest you focus on anything else; I pay you for this reason, that you would take care for nothing else. Keep watch, and focus on nothing else, *be anxious about nothing.*[472] So that you don't lose the care you ought to have regarding this, focus on nothing else." But turn it around: "By caring for estate and honor and the things of the body, you have no care for the things of the soul; you don't remember what fulfills the salvation of your soul." That's typical.

Jesus Christ so much wants to warn you and make you understand and seat in your memory how much this matters to you, and that you should only live for this, that your life itself is called a *watch*, because you live for this; and if you don't do it, what are you living for? The care that you have for this is so great that the ages of men are called *vigils*: childhood, first vigil; youth is called second; young manhood,[473] the third, and so on. Let those of you who do not understand this language learn it, with Christ burdening us, with Christ teaching us that we are to live for this, for keeping watch. He calls life a "watch": the boy keeps watch, and the young man keeps watch, and the old man keeps watch, and all the life of men is nothing else but a perpetual watch. All of life is a watch: what will become of him who sleeps all his life? What will become of him? Why so much sleep? How many of us here are keeping watch and saying, "Lord, if You are served by it, and I die tonight, I am very content; I am prepared!" You sleep? If the bridegroom comes tonight and says, "Walk over here," what would you do? If you heard, "Walk over here, for your days are finished," what would you feel, what would your stomach do to you? If that powerful voice of

---

472 *Nihil solliciti sitis*. Phil 4:6.

473 *Mocedad* is defined as encompassing the time between puberty and adulthood; in modern terms, it might apply to the teenager and young adult years.

God sounded forth, what would we do? I believe that, if we heard it, we would walk about like crazy people: "Run, call so-and-so to me, pay back that one, make the other whole, pay that debt." What carelessness, what sleep, how asleep we are! Do you dare to lie down in sin? And if you die, what will become of you? And if you go to hell, what will become of you?

God commands us to keep watch, and we sleep, and lest, at some time, God comes to you, be on guard, don't lie down and fall asleep again. Don't you understand that, if God has awakened you, you have to be on watch, so that you don't go back to sleep? He whom God has awoken must take as much care as he who sleeps. I speak to the novices, my brothers. If God has come into your heart, if He has awoken you—"God has moved my heart in such a way that whatever I left in the world isn't worth a straw to me"—I believe you. And although there were a thousand worlds, he has encountered a good that has all goods. See how all evils will not make him fall, having this great good. I want you to always keep awake, brothers. See how bitter it is to know God and to offend Him; see how it hurts to enjoy Him and to lose Him; see how strong His wrath feels. You were sleeping, He called you at Matins, you did not wake, you did not hear Him, you did not go there. The fault is easy to gloss over. That fault has an excuse, you couldn't do more; but if they called you and, awake, you heard them calling you to Matins, and you did not go, and you went back to sleep, that is a great evil. How evil, you will know later!

You say: Where is my God? He frees us. He who has sought God and has found Him, let him guard Him well; let him beseech Him and throw two thousand prayers at Him; let him throw a thousand bonds at Him; let him set a thousand guards before Him; the greatest caution, the greatest diligence is needed in order not to sleep. All of life has to be a vigil. *Keep vigil, therefore.*[474] It is a very high business, it is a business of very great difficulty, to serve

---

[474] *Vigilate itaque.*

God. What business is there that is higher, that is more arduous? That is one of the hidden mysteries of God. And let no one tell you that it is enough to serve God as you wish, that God does not ask for such strictures, that what you wish is enough. God willing, we'll put that to the test! God willing, you'll take up arms! There is nothing easier for the man who has not been to war than to boast about it and about arms, to tell the people stories of war. The other, who knows it, laughs at him. It is a business that needs great caution, great diligence, and because of this, Jesus Christ thus declared, "So if there is someone who tells you, 'Go on, you're joking, whatever you want's enough,' don't believe him, don't let them deceive you." Is it a little matter for some men that we are called to shine like the sun—*The just will shine like the sun*[475]—to give light like the stars?

A Great Lord Requires a Great Service

Like the stars shining in the darkness of night, so Christians are to shine among other peoples, among other nations, and, among Christians, the religious are to shine more, for they are to be always at vigil, and among the religious, those of the order of the glorious . . . Who is a better watcher than our father?, etc.[476] We men who are called to do good, to love our friends and enemies, to suffer blows and not avenge ourselves, to be pure—does this seem to us like a little thing, like a little matter? "Does God ask so much of those who follow Him?" Yes: since He is a great King, a great service is owed Him, and He wants to be highly served. Let the novices, my brothers—for I'm talking to them—see what master they have entered into service with. When we are baptized, we establish our-

---

475 *Fulgebunt iusti sicut sol.* Mt 13:43.

476 These lines seem to have been left incomplete in the manuscript. St. John probably wrote this sermon as a template to give at various monasteries, leaving a spot here to praise the founder of whichever order the particular monastery belonged to.

selves as servants of that great Lord, of that great King, *for a great God and great king is the Lord.*[477] A great lord requires a great service. One establishes himself with a great prince: what care one has for what he says, for what he does, for his person, for his customs! However great be the majesty of this Lord, so great is the offense done against Him. No sin can be small against so great a Lord. Saint Jerome: *Although it is not a light thing to offend God, even in light matters, yet he is most prudent who considers not so much the breadth of the empire as the majesty of the emperor.*[478] Death before offending so great a Lord! A most high lord asks for a most high service. It is not licit to think otherwise; if one is in choir, he is before so great a Lord; if in prayer, [he is] like someone speaking with the Lord; if at Mass, [he is] like someone who is making offerings to the great majesty of God. If you do anything whatsoever, think that you are serving such a Lord, who wants to be most highly served in everything. And He makes such a fuss about our staying awake so that the great good He gained for us, the many labors that He suffered for us, would not be in vain.

Let our minds understand how great a thing it is that God became man for men, that He was affronted and lashed, etc., for us. Oh brothers, and how great a danger there is here! God commands me to serve Him. So that man would learn, the true Master comes to teach. He comes to serve men, so that men would learn to serve God, not like the masters of the law who speak, teaching by word and not by work. Lord, may You Yourself help us by Your mercy, so that Your good would not become evil for us, Your medicine

---

477 *Quoniam Deus magnus Dominus et rex magnus.* Ps 95:3.

478 *Quamquam leve non sit Deum et levibus offendere, ille quam prudentissimus est qui non tam quantitatem imperii considerat quam majestatem imperantis.* See St. Jerome, *Epistle* CXLVIII.6: "And I really don't know if we could call any sin 'light' when it is committed in contempt of God. And he is most prudent who does not so much consider what is ordered as much as Him Who orders it, nor thinks as much of the breadth of the empire as of the dignity of the emperor" (PL 22:1207).

not become poison for us, Your sweetness not [become] gall and bitterness! If God, in His majesty, lowered Himself so much, with what face will a little worm so puff himself up with pride and command? How? Seeing his Lord lower Himself to serve His servants, who will not serve Him, who will despise Him? Then how are you embarrassed to serve your neighbors for Jesus Christ, who served all for you? Seeing your God so poor that He sometimes, for hunger, gleaned the ears of grain in the fields to eat, why does the slave want to enrich himself with good and bad, with licit and illicit dealings? Seeing the labors that Jesus Christ suffered in His body for you, with what face are you thinking of your delights of the flesh, of your bed, while the eyes of God see your filthy deeds? Do you dare to call yourself Christian, Christ having put His body out in the cold and labors for you, and you, when you have a little bit of cold, [say], "give me the hides, the furs," running away from looking like Christ, running away from what we need to do to be Christians? Oh, shame of Christians! The body of Jesus Christ was so maltreated, and that of His servants and slaves is so regaled! What do we have to do with Jesus Christ? How are we like Jesus Christ? Let us understand it through your life. How should we understand it? The Son of the Virgin *did not come to be served, but to serve.*[479] May the angels bless You for this, Lord! "And through what service, and in what ways, do You want to serve and have You served?" *By giving His soul*;[480] by giving all of Himself, by dying for us. A boy serves you with spurs, you pay him; another with shield, you pay him. And You, Lord, have served us by giving Your life for us. May the heavens bless You. Amen. Pardon us, Lord, by who You are. He came to serve so that we might learn to serve, so that you would burn with love every time you see Jesus Christ serving you, pouring forth His blood for you.

479 Mt 20:28.

480 *Dare animam suam.*

Let Us Represent the Death of Christ in Our Life

If there were a woman who, during the eight days of burial rites for her husband, commanded her children to play and joke and ride on carriages, and she with them, and [commanded] that there be parties and festivals, what would you say? Wouldn't this seem a monstrous thing, and wouldn't such a loveless and faithless woman be cruel? All would say: "You well show that you don't love your husband." Beg Our Lord so that we ourselves would not be worse than her. Are we not at Christ's funeral? Are we not at the time when, each day, the Church represents His death and burial to us? Do you think that we're at Easter parties? Do you think that we're at feasts? We are only at the burial. Say, by your life, if God had told all of us who are here that we are to be saved, most certainly, what security would we have that we would have [salvation]? Being in such great danger of perdition, remember, keep watch, see how we are not at Easter parties, we are not safe; we are in danger, we walk in war, we have not yet arrived at the gate. We celebrate the funeral rites of Christ. It is the time of the Passion, we sing the Mass of Requiem.[481] Saint Paul says, *Don't you know that whoever of you has been baptized with Christ, we have also been buried with Christ through His death?*[482] *Don't you know that, when they baptized us, they buried us with Jesus Christ,* so that we might know that we represent His death in our life and that we have to live like someone whose old man is dead? Because of this, the religious wear habits that look like the dead.

---

[481] The feast of Saint Catherine—the nominal occasion for this sermon—is on November 25, and the month of November is dedicated to praying for the repose of souls, often through the saying of votive Requiem Masses.

[482] *An nescitis, quod quicumque baptizati estis cum Christo, ac sepulti sumus cum Christo per mortem ipsius.* Rom 6:3–4.

Saint Paul says, *But I bear the mortification of Jesus Christ in my body.*[483] "What is that?" Stones, lashes, insults, persecutions: this is to carry Jesus Christ in one's body.

"What? Do we always have to carry the mortification of Jesus Christ in our bodies? What is this?"

"Always"—as Saint Paul says it—means, Christian, that, while sleeping, keeping awake, night and day, in prosperity and in adversity, it behooves us to carry Jesus Christ in our souls, so that we would always carry on war in the flesh with pride, etc. Each day we represent the honors, the funeral rites of the Passion of Jesus Christ. It is not the time for honors, it is not the time for feasts, it is not the time for rests. But if, during the time in which you are to celebrate these funeral rites, you go on carriage rides, you go on pleasure walks, it is a sign that you do not love, it is a sign that you do not feel His death; it well seems like you don't understand it. Jesus Christ poured forth His blood for your good. Jesus Christ died for you, and you will take evil from it, you will take your condemnation from it, through doing so great an evil.

The sluggard hides his hands under his . . ., etc.[484] (Read it there, by your life.) It is the lazy hand upon hand, and its laziness is such that it seems like it will consume the estate. Is this not a great evil? See how far we have come, how much we have gone down, for it is not enough that we are lazy in labor, that we have our hands hidden, but we even don't want to eat. Brother, if it seems to you that you are delicate, that you don't have the strength to suffer five thousand lashes, to suffer such hunger, such cold, to pour forth so much blood, at the least, have enough [strength] to carry the food you have to your mouth. If you don't have the strength to labor, don't have the laziness of the dead at home, so that you would take advantage of another's labor. For He having passed by—blessed be He!— having

---

483 *Ego autem, mortificationem Iesu Christi porto in corpore meo.* 2 Cor 4:10; Gal 6:17.

484 *Abscondit piger manus suas sub sua . . .,* etc. Prv 19:24; 26:15.

arranged the medicine, having prepared such a stew, we don't want to carry it to our mouth, nor take advantage of it. Whatever comes to me from His hand, that is what fulfills me and with which I am very content. But how do we not have the strength to receive, how do we have such laziness in receiving, the Sacraments, since, through them, we are given the strength of Jesus Christ? Run, confess; run, take that bread of life. They'll say to you: "Leave off, since Lent's coming." Even until the food's in your mouth, you are lazy! You will beg, and they won't give to you; you *will ask for oil*, when the stores are already closed.

"Let us run to that deceitful thing for protection"; our wall is made of worn-out reeds, so that, at the time when it needs to stand firm, it will shatter; but, *if the Lord* does not guard *the house, in vain does he who* guards it *labor.*[485] How many of us here are keeping awake? How many are at peace with their conscience? How many would say, if God called me tonight, "we'll go willingly," "I'm prepared"? What remedy for such sleepiness? I don't know any other except our going to the vastness of the mercy of Christ, our throwing ourselves at His feet. Let us go to those merciful hands, let us tell Him: "Lord, when You walked in the world and they brought You a blind man, You looked at him, You cast Your blessing upon him; then look at me, Lord, for I come here to Your mercy. My soul is more paralytic than their bodies; I am blind for seeing You; I am lame for walking the steps of my salvation; I have withered hands for doing good works; I am deaf for hearing Your words and my good; I am mute for Your praises. Heal me, Lord!" I don't know another remedy. When they give someone a stabbing, later, when he feels it, he goes to the doctor's feet; let us go, then, to the feet of Doctor Jesus Christ: "Lord, how our days have been spent! Lord, how sleeping am I! Remedy me." And I don't know any other remedy for keeping awake except our going to the Son of God and pleading

[485] Ps 127:1.

Him so that, since He always keeps awake—*Behold, He will not sleep nor slumber*[486]—He would awaken our sleep, revive our care.

Martyrdom of Saint Catherine

Today is the feast of the blessed Saint Catherine. How did she get oil? A very rich maiden, very wise, very beautiful, and of great lineage; yet, because of the great madness she had, she didn't want to marry anyone; and, through this, God lashed her.[487] It was put in her heart that He—Jesus Christ—and no other, was richer and wiser, and better, and more beautiful than her. Christ told her, when they brandished knives at her, "I will not forsake you." What a consolation those words gave her when they insulted her, when they lashed her! Saint Paul felt lashes and stones. For he set in a balance all those labors, and the one saying of Jesus Christ: "Walk on, Paul, for I will be with you." Without comparison, that word consoled her more than the lashes for Jesus Christ's sake gave her pain. Her consolation would come later. Are we full of the consolations of the world? Then the consolations of God do not come to such as us. How *blessed are those who weep, for they*, and no others, *will be consoled*![488] Having read the sentence, that they would slit her throat, she gave thanks to her bridegroom Jesus Christ. As Cyprian[489] read the sentence, she gave thanks to God and said, "Oh my Lord, crown of virgins, strength of the dead, succor of those

---

486 *Ecce non dormitabit neque dormiet.* Ps 121:4.

487 The meaning seems to be that this is the means by which God struck her heart and converted her, but it is odd that St. John used the harsh word *lashed* (*azotó*), which he later used to describe her torture.

488 Mt 5:4.

489 "Cyprian" seems to be St. John's rendition of the name "Chursates"; in the Latin *Passion of Saint Catherine of Alexandria* §22, this is the name of the "prefect of the city and very man of Belial" who devised St. Catherine's torture wheel. St. Catherine's cry of joy is based on what she says in the Latin *Passion of Saint Catherine of Alexandria* §24.

in tribulation!" And the sword [blow] fell, and a jet of milk came forth, to denote that she was pure, that she was most chaste, and that she was all white like a dove. Her body was buried on Mount Sinai. A stream of oil flowed forth. Doesn't it seem to you that the blessed women had received oil? Her soul was presented by the angels in glory, *which may Jesus, son of Mary, deign to bestow upon me and you.*[490] Amen.

490 *Quam mihi et vobis praestare dignetur Iesus filius Mariae.*